AF531627

PROBLEMS OF CONTINUING EDUCATION

PROBLEMS OF CONTINUING EDUCATION

By

V. JANARDHANA RAO

DISCOVERY PUBLISHING HOUSE
NEW DELHI-1100 02

First Published–2000
Reprint : 2012
ISBN 81-7141-544-X

© Author

DISCOVERY PUBLISHING HOUSE
4831/24, Ansari Road, Prahlad Street,
Darya Ganj, New Delhi-110002 (India)
Phone: 3279245 · Fax: 91-11-3253475

E-mail:dph@indiatimes.com

Printed at:
Dynamic Printers

ACKNOWLEDGEMENTS

I express my sincere gratitude to my guide Dr. B .Niranjan Reddy, Professor, Department of Adult Education S.V. University, Tirupati, for his guidance and encouragement during the period of present investigation.

I wish to regard my sincere thanks to Dr. P.A. Reddy, Project Officer in the Department of Adult Education, S.V. University, Tirupati for his constant encouragement and valuable guidance throughout my M. Phil, programme.

My sincere thanks to our Head of the Department Dr. M. V. Sudhakara Reddy, Director, Department of Adult Education, S.V. University, Tirupati.

I am also grateful to all the Adult Education Supervisors, Monitors and Neo-literates for their co-operation and assistance in collection of the data.

My heartiest thanks to Dr. G. Lakanadha Reddy, Lecturer in Education, Alagappa University, Tamilnadu and Dr. T. Kumaraswamy, Project Officer, Department of Adult Education, S.V. University, Tirupati.

I am grateful to colleagues of the faculty Dr. S. Khadir Basha. Mr. Ananda Reddy, Dr. Reddy Basha, Mr. Ramana Reddy and Mr. G. Reddeppa.

I owe a deep sense of gratitude to my friends and relatives.

Finally I am very much thankful to Sri. A. Veera Ragavaiah, Rtd., Head Master, who took language correction of my dissertation and Mr. S. Bhaskar Reddy who took up Computer work neatly and accurately.

V. Janardhana Rao
Tirupati

CONTENTS

1

INTRODUCTION

TOTAL LITERACY - CONCEPT, MEANING AND IMPORTANCE

Recognising the relationship between the rate of literacy and socio-economic development of the society, a large number of least developed countries have given prominent place for Adult Education Programme in their budgets. As a result, Adult Education Programmes of different kinds are conceived and are being implemented throughout the world. This is also true in the case of India. Government of India has launched a massive National Adult Education Programme in 1978 to cover the 100 million illiterates within a span of five years. However, it was reviewed during 1980 and incorporated in the new 20 point programme for effective implementation. Again the programme was revised, strengthened and launched in the name of National Literacy Mission in 1988 for making 100 million illiterates into functional literates by 1997. The National Literacy Mission programme has adopted mass campaign approach for total literacy through mass participation and voluntarism for eradication of illiteracy.

As a test case for total literacy, the Ernakulam literacy project was sanctioned for eradication of total illiteracy. The success of Ernakulam project paved a way for launching Total Literacy Campaigns throughout the country for imparting functional literacy under the aegis of *Zilla Saksharatha Samithis* constituted at District level. As a part of Total Literacy Campaign in different districts of different states. Chittoor district is one of the first district to implement Total Literacy Campaign in Rayalaseema region of Andhra Pradesh. The campaign was launched on 2nd October, 1990 to cover 6.25 lakhs of illiterates in the age group of 9 to 35 years. However, 5.44 lakhs participated and attended the centres. As per the external evaluation 86.7 per cent of literacy was achieved. As a result of successful implementation of Total Literacy Campaigns, a new situation emerged where by millions of literates are acquiring basic literacy skills and joining the class of Neo-literates each year.

Post Literacy - Concept, Meaning and Importance

The experience in the field of Adult Education in India as well as in other countries shows that in the absence of learning environment and effective programme of post-literacy and continuing education, the efforts made in literacy programme yield extremely limited results. Recognising the above, the National Policy on Education and Programme of Action (1986) has given considerable attention to the need for creation of satisfactory arrangements for post-literacy and continuing education. Further, the National Policy on Education (N. P. E.) envisaged the comprehensive programme of post-literacy and continuing education for the neo-literates and the youth who have received primary education with a view to enable them to retain and upgrade their literacy skills and to harness it for the improvement of their living and working conditions. Further, N. P. E. also stresses the importance of post-literacy and continuing education for the Neo-literates so that they are prevented from relapsing into illiteracy. With this object in view, the Govt. of India has launched the scheme of Jana Shikshana Nilayams (JSN) in February, 1988 to cover all over the country in a phased manner. The aim of the scheme is to institutionalise the post-literacy and continuing education and to ensure retention of literacy skills, provision of facilities to enable the learners to continuing their learning beyond elementary level and to create scope for application of their learning for improvement of their living conditions. However, the specific objective of the scheme of JSNs are as follows.

1. Provision of facilities for retention, continuing education and application of functional literacy.

2. Dissemination of information on development programmes, widening and improving participation of traditionally deprived sections of society.
3. Creation of awareness about national concerns such as national integration, conservation and improvement of the environment, women's equality, observance of small family norm etc. and sharing of common problems of the community.
4. Improvement of economic condition and general well being as well as improvement of productivity.
5. Recreation and healthy living.

In order to achieve the above objectives, the JSN are performing the following functions.

i) Evening Class : For upgradation of literacy and numeral skills to be organised for 3-4 hours once a week. The learners would have the option to come for an hour or so at their convenience.
ii) Library : For this books would be purchased from the non-recurring and recurring provisions. Copies of old journals will be maintained and use of booklets relating to development programmes will be provided.
iii) Reading Room: With wall papers, and news papers appropriate for adult learners, informative and entertaining journals, developmental literature etc.
iv) Churcha Mandal: Discussion group for decision on common problems.
v) Training Programmes: Simple and of short duration relating to health and family welfare, new developments in agriculture and animal husbandry conservation of energy etc. J.S.N may also help the local youth to benefit from various vocational training programmes.
vi) Sports and Adventurous Activities: The stress being laid on indigenous sports, walking, excursions, cycling trips in groups, visit to development projects etc.
vii) Recreation and Cultural Activities : Particularly traditional and folk forms of art, rural theatre, puppetry etc.
viii) Information Window : For securing information on various developmental programmes, information and material suitable for neo-literates have to be procured from the concerned development agencies.

ix) Communication Centre : Where community radio, audio cassette player-cum recorder may be provided.

Each JSN will cover about 5,000 population spread over in a cluster of 4 to 5 villages. The JSNs in view of their broad scope of operation will cover various categories of persons viz.

1. The neo-literates who complete the functional literacy course;
2. Those who become literate through the mass programme for functional literacy;
3. School dropouts;
4. Passouts of primary schools;
5. Passouts of Nonformal Education programme; and
6. all the other members of the community so far as group activities and cultural programmes are concerned.

Each JSN will be manned by a person called *prerak*. The prerak is one who volunteers to spare sometime and serve the community with a spirit of service. However, the JSN has suggested some parameters for the selection of persons as *preraks*.

The parameters are as follows:

1. Must be from local area;
2. have given evidence of interest in serving the community, particularly women and economically deprived sections of the society;
3. have leadership quality and ability to take voluntary help of the local youth;
4. have sufficient freetime, atleast 3-4 hours every evening;
5. be atleast a Matriculate, (to be reduced to VIII class level in respect of specially gifted persons, women and persons belonging to SC/ST).

In order to implement the various activities of the J.S.N. the prerak has to perform the following functions.

1) to run the activities of a J. S. N. cited above, himself/herself with the help of volunteers.
2) to organise post-literacy and continuing education programmes in the villages other than the ones in which J.S.N. is situated (and which are under his supervisory responsibility), *inter-alia*, by

— taking news papers, journals and books at the time of his visit to those villages.

— organising inter-village sports and cultural competitions,

— inviting interested persons for interaction with development functionaries etc.,

— encouraging local youth/women to take responsibility as honorary J.S.N. extension workers.

3. to supervise adult education centres and /or non-formal education centres. It is expected that the *Prerak* will run the J.S.N. activities for 3 days in a week. Necessary provision for this has been made in the scheme of Rural Functional Literacy Projects and Presumably also in State Adult Education projects.

The National Literacy Mission (N.L.M) envisaged that after achieving Total Literacy Campaign (T..L.C.) in each of the district, there must be a provision for post literacy and continuing education activities. This provision is made in the form of establishing a good number of JCKs in each of the T..L.C. districts declared.

Concept of J.C.Ks. For Post-Literacy Activities

In Chittoor district, the T..L.C. was launched on 2nd October, 1990 and 5.44 Lakh people participated and attended the centre as per the external evaluation. The evaluation revealed that 86.7% of the literacy was achieved.

In view of the emergence of large pool of Neo-literates, 10,000 *Jana Chaithanya Kendras* (JCKs) were established to cover the neo-literates, semi-literates, school drop-outs, non formal education dropouts and all those who wish to continue their education in the village/area on the lines of JSNs. The only difference between the JCK and JSN is that the incharge of centre is called monitor and he is a volunteer without any remuneration. The goals and objectives of the post-literacy programme of chittoor district is as follows.

1. Covering the leftover learners in basic literacy.
2. Consolidating and stabilising the literacy skills of neo-literates.
3. Upgrading the skills of semi-literates to minimum literacy levels.

4. Formulation of neoliterate books which are suitably graded and adult education oriented.
5. Achieving the transition from neoliteracy to autonomous learning through reading materials at increased level of literacy.
6. Striving for autonomous learning among all learners towards creative lifelong learning.
7. Consolidating the awareness generated about social issues and to organise people on that basis.
8. Providing opportunities for self development among the neoliterates in the fields of their choice.
9. Establishing institutions for formal/non-formal/informal education, for continuing education and thereby enrich the learning environment.
10. Identifying and training the volunteers who work as agents in these institutions.

Roles and Functions of the Monitors of JCKs

The success of the JCKs largely depends on the monitors who are the incharge of the JCKs. As a post literacy worker, the monitor has to play the multiple roles in different marked situations. These multiple roles demand a variety of capabilities on the part of the monitors. As the word monitor itself reveals that he/she has to organise the centre for both literacy as well as post-literacy activities, mobilising the material as well as human resources to upgrade the functional information and skills of the learners on varied occupations and giving guidance and counselling to the people and the learners where the JCK is located.

Each JCK is manned by two monitors. Monitors are Volunteers working on non-remunirative basis. As per the T.L.C. of Chittoor district, the qualities of a JCK monitor are

a. be settled in life and not looking for opportunities for employment.
b. be in the age group of 20-40 years.
c. have worked as volunteer in the Akshara Tapasman programme.
d. have passed/failed atleast 10th class.
e. not belong to any political party.

f. have the willingness and ability to organise people.
g. have progressive ideas and be prepared to work on long term basis for the education and training of adults.

The successful implementation of the JCK largely depends upon the achievement of the objectives for which it is created. Further, as already stated, the achievement of objectives also lies on the successful performance of the functions prescribed to the monitor. The functions of the monitor as per T.L.C. of Chittoor District are as follows.

1. Enabling the neo-literates to read fourth primer (*Maanava Jeevanam*), daily newspapers and forthnightly (*Velugubata*).
2. Helping the droputs and absentees of the literacy, phase to complete the three primers.
3. Motivating learners to attend JCKs.
4. Writing the news highlights on the literacy wall from local news papers in regional language.
5. Providing books (Monthlies, weeklies, story books etc.,) to neo-literates from State Resource Centre for Adult Education, Hyderabad or Zilla Saksharatha Samithi, Chittoor.
6. Organising simple and short duration training programmes, sports and cultural activities, picnics/visits to government offices and other places.
7. Strengthening and utilising the services of village Adult Education Committees for JCKs.
8. Organising the churcha mandals and village parliaments.
9. Pursuing neo-literates and others to send their children to school.
10. Securing the co-operation of village elite, Mahila Mandals, youth clubs in organising the activities of JCK.
11. Disseminating the information on development programmes and about the circulars of ZSS to JCK participants.
12. Participating in the training programmes and the post-literacy campaigns, padayatras, afforestation, family planning, small savings, cleanliness campaigns and review meetings.
13. Reporting the performance of JCKs to ZSS.
14. Helping the resource organisations, agencies, associations with education, training, research and extension activities.

Problems of Monitors in Jana Chaithanya Kendras

As a JCK monitor, the monitor's activities are diversified in nature, in marked situations. He/she has to do the activities related to organisation of JCKs, management and administration of JCKs, and environment building in JCK for conducive learning. These activities inturn demand co-operative attitude on the part of the monitor to procure a variety of materials from the developmental agencies both Government and Non-government for the promotion of functional literacy as well as upgradation of vocational skills among the learners and the community people. In doing all these activities, the JCK monitor may come across several problems relating to the Organisation, Administration, Environment building and Mobilising Human and Material resources for effective functioning of JCKs.

The organisational problems may be such as choosing a convenient place, lighting facilities for JCks, providing need based activities for the learners, motivating dropouts and neo-literates to continue their education and paying special attention for slow and backward learners and so on. Several administrative problems like constituting village literacy committee, inadequate training for effective implementation of JCKs, lack of recognition for monitors from the higherups, age variation between the monitors and local leaders in dealing with the common problems, lack of training and experience among the monitors in conducting cultural programmes and lack of skills in identification of learning problems of learners and so on may hamper the programme.

Similarly, problems related to the environmental aspects of JCKs such as, village politics, caste and religion variations, non-availability of the suitable place for organisation of sports and games, blind beliefs and customs in the village relating to women education may hinder the JCK activities. On the otherhand, the problems such as maintaining human relations with the village leaders by the JCK monitors, lack of skill in maintaining report with the developmental department, inadequate skills in organisation of Charcha Mandals and implementation of their decisions etc., may lead to low performance of the JCK monitors.

From the conceptual structure of the JCK, one can easily understand that the success of the JCK largely depends on the way in which the JCK monitor pool and co-ordinate the human and material resources both for organisation and administrative as well as academic purposes. In doing this major activity, the monitor may come across the problem such as lack of suitable literacy material for the promotion of literacy, irregular supply of newspapers to JCKs for the promotion of reading habits in the neo-literates, lack of audio-visual aids in JCKs, non-availability of the materials to suit the varied interest of the learners, the higher standard of the books available in JCKs, lack of provision for the production of posters and charts in propagating JCK activities and insufficient information on the varied developmental programmes that are implemented by the Government and Non-government agencies for he development of weaker sections and so on.

Keeping an eye on the likely problems to be faced by the JCK monitors and identification of such problems and finding out the possible ways and means to overcome such problems will naturally facilitate the activities of the JCK monitors.

Need for Identification of the Problems of the Monitors in JCKs of Post-Literacy Programmes

In view of the above it clearly appears that successful implementation of JCKs largely depends on the qualities, capabilities and functional ability of the monitors. As already stated the multi dimensional activities of JCKs. demand the monitor to perform various functions, activities and he has to interact with heterogenious groups of the society. In this process, the Monitor has to face innumerable problems both personal and professional and has to overcome these problems with tact. In order to make his job easy, it was suggested to identify and prepare a list of anticipated problems of Monitors while discharging the duties. The identification of the problems not only helps the Monitor to tackle them easily but also helps him to improve his efficiency. It also helps the trainers to equip the perspective Monitors and working Monitors. Keeping this in view, the present investigation for identification of the problems of the Monitors in discharging their duties was formulated. The study is not only intended to identify the problems and to study the associations between the problems and personal characteristics of the monitors.

2

REVIEW OF LITERATURE

REVIEW OF RELATED RESEARCH

In any scientific investigation, the review of literature helps the researcher to know the researches done in that particular area/topic. The clear picture on the researches already completed and the gaps that are existing or the uncovered aspects of the area will pave better insight into the problem to be investigated by the researcher. In other sense the review of literature will make the researcher's efforts more profitable, effective and time saving. Keeping the above rationale in mind the researcher reviewed the studies relating to the present topic under study.

The available and relevant studies are review and presented under three headings, viz.,

2.1. Studies on the TLC.
2.2. Studies on the JSN.
2.3. Studies on the Problems of the Post-literacy workers.

Studies on the TLC

An Evaluation of Literacy Campaign of Chittoor District of A.P. was done by University of Hyderabad and the National Institute of Rural Development, Hyderabad (1992). The study revealed that:

1. 77.9 per cent of the sample learners qualified in the test as per the EEA norms.
2. The Achievement rate of the male learners was 76.9 per cent, while that of the females 78.85 per cent.
3. The performance of SCs learners was particularly good. About 80 per cent of the SCs learners became neo-literates in comparison to 78 per cent of the STs and 74 per cent of the backward classes and 79 per cent of the other classes.
4. The literacy campaign in Chittoor on the whole appears to have evoked a better response among women than the men. Their achievement rate was 78.85 per cent in comparison to 76.9 per cent of the male neo- literates.
5. The literacy Primer 1,II, III being used in the campaign and found many deficiencies in these books and concluded that if better material was provided to the learners, the result of the campaign would have been still better.

Saldana (1992) evaluated the LIteracy Campaign in Warda district and the findings of the study were as follows;

1. The learners scoring data was divided into four grades *i.e.*, A, B, C, D. 1.76 per cent of the tested sample achieved grade A with 60 per cent and above marks, 15.4 per cent Grade B with 45 to 59 per cent marks, 2.7 per cent grade C with 35 to 45 marks and 5.7 per cent achieved grade D scoring less than 35 per cent marks.
2. Both males and females generally scored higher marks in numeracy as compared to their respective performance in reading and writing. 67.9 per cent of the males and 60.7 per cent of the females attained grade A in numeracy as against 28 per cent and 20.2 per cent in reading and writing respectively. The mean scores of the total sample in numeracy were 76.17 per cent as against that in reading and writing.
3. The overall achievement on the cut-off-point prescribed by EET *i.e.*, scoring of 35 per cent marks in aggregate was 99.4 per cent in case of males and 93.1 per cent in case of females. The achievement of SCs and STs was 98.4 per cent and 95.9 per cent respectively. The mean scores of successful candidates in reading, writing and numeracy were 73.42, 43.39 and 76.66 per cent respectively.

4. The achievement of the sample learners according to the NLM norms as later calculated comes to 47.24 per cent, 52.2 per cent for males, 44.1 per cent for females and 46.0 per cent in case of Scheduled castes and Scheduled Tribes.

Indra Deva and Rajasekhar (1993) evaluated the TLC in Bilaspur of Madhya Pradesh state. The results of the study indicates that

1. 74 per cent of the learners reached the NLM norms.
2. The scheduled caste learners provided a very good outcome in two sub-projects, namely, Matsuri and Pamgarlu with 91 per cent and 87 per cent success, the third project Seepat came out with the success of 54 per cent only.
3. Among tribal sub-projects, Belghana, Kota, Pali and Haridibazar provided a success rate of 85 per cent 83 and 67 per cent respectively.
4. Average score secured by the successful learners in reading, writing and numeracy were 81, 66 and 87 per cent respectively.

Evaluation of literacy campaign in Jalna was conducted by Deshpande (1993) of Indian Institute of Education and the findings of the study were as follows:

1. In the sample evaluation 20,109 learners appeared in the test and 17,781 were found qualified according to the NLM norms, providing an overall result of 88.42 per cent. The pass per centage of the male was 89.20 per cent and the female 88.04 per cent.
2. The scoring of the marks, the average scores of both male and female were almost same i.e., 81.17 per cent and 80.65 per cent respectively which proved that female learners in Jalna district were equally competent as the male learners.
3. The performance of young learners in the age group 9.14 in the district was as good as or in some cases little better, than that of the adult learners.
4. In the corporative performance of total learners in reading, writing and numeracy, it was found that writing ability with 72.23 per cent mean scores was the lowest as compared to numerical ability with 83.96 mean scores and writing ability with 30.2 mean scores.

Rokadiya (1993) evaluated the TLC of Ajmer (Rajastan). The following are the findings of the evaluation. Out of the total of 6,694 learners evaluated, 4,536 or 85.01 per cent achieved level 'A' (with 80 per cent and above marks), 695 or 10.85 per cent achieved level 'C' (with 60-69 per cent marks thus, the total outcome of the external evaluation was 89.22 per cent.

Prem chand (1993) evaluated the TLC of Dungarpur in Rajasthan and the findings were as follows:

1. Out of the 3891 learners who appeared in the test 3574 (91.9%) achieved level 'A' scoring more than 70 per cent of marks, 272 (7.0%) scoring 50 to 70 per cent marks and 45 (1.1%) achieved level 'C' scoring less than 50 per cent marks. Out of the achievers of Grade 'A', 1155 out of 1220 were males and 2419 out of 2,671 were females.
2. Achievements in different literacy abilities 90.5%, 87.6% and 76.3% of the learners achieved grade 'A' in numeracy, reading and writing respectively.
3. Age group-wise achievements of learners 55.17 per cent in the age-group 6-9, 90.39% in the age group 9-14 and 92.29% in the age group 15-40 achieved grade 'A'.
4. In the projected total targeted age-group 6-40 in the sample villages/urban areas, the percentage of those who secured grade 'a' comes to 55.3 per cent and to the available learners it comes to 73.92 per cent (males 76.85 per cent and females 72.60 per cent).
5. The literacy rate of the District is expected to have gone up from 80.55 per cent in 1991 to more than 50 per cent in 1993.

Tata Institute of Social Sciences (1993) evaluated the TLC in Lathur. The evaluation reveals the following.

About 82 per cent of the evaluated learners scored above 50 per cent marks in the literacy test, the achievement 82 per cent of the learners succeeded as per the EET norms and 49.7 per cent as per the National Literacy Norms. As per the NLM norms 58.4 per cent of the males, 45.2 per cent of females, 51.6 per cent of the learners in rural areas and 38.95 per cent of the learners in the urban areas succeeded in the test. The success of SCs and STs was 46 per cent performance in the 3 components of reading, writing and numeracy.

It was found that the mean performance was good in numeracy than in reading and writing.

Tata Institute of Social Sciences evaluated the TLCs in Nanded (Maharashtra) 1993. The findings of this study were:

The learning outcome on the basis of literacy test was 82.7%, 58.8% for all the learners, tested by EET. 90.8 per cent of males evaluated were declared qualified according to the EET norms and 70.7 per cent according to the NLM norms, (61.8 per cent of the learners scored more than 70 per cent marks, 20.9 per cent 50 to 70 per cent marks respectively). The achievement rate of SCs, ST and Minority communities comes to 58.8 per cent. The achievements in different literacy abilities of reading, writing and numeracy of 81.2 per cent, 75.5 per cent and 82.7 per cent respectively scored 50 per cent or more marks. Overall achievement of literacy campaign is 41.90 per cent. In terms of the number of months of learning, those who had less than six months of learning, performed poor as compared to those who had more than six months of instruction.

The NIRD evaluated the Literacy Campaign in Chittoor District (1994). The study reveals the following learning outcomes.

1. The cut-off points for declaring the learner successful in the test was taken as 50 per cent deviating from the NLMA norms in scoring 70 per cent in aggregate and 50 per cent marks in each of the reading, writing and numeracy abilities. Thus 81.6 per cent of the sample learners were found successful in the literacy test. With regards to the division-wise analysis, 95.38 per cent success rate was recorded in Chittoor division, followed by 77.8 per cent in Madanapalli and 71.2 per cent in Tirupati division.
2. The average score for the entire sample was 67.27 (63.82 in case of females and 71.85 in case of males), the mean scores of scheduled castes, scheduled tribes and backward classes was found to be 64.87, 61.55, 66.86 and 72.10 respectively.
3. It was found that female agricultural labourers secured less marks than their counterparts.
4. Marital status of the learners has not either impeded or improved the learning process of the learners.

Zakir (1994) evaluated the Total Literacy campaign of Yamunanagar, a district of Haryana state. The findings of the study discloses that out of the 337 sample learners tested by EET, 167 passed the test on the NLM norms providing an overall achievement of 48.18 per cent and most of the learners were found poor in reading, writing and numeracy. The overall performance of the actual learners appearing for the test is not very encouraging.

Om Mehta and others (1994) evaluated the literacy campaign in Durg of Madhya Pradesh state. The results of the study shows that 80 per cent of the rural learners and 72.01 per cent of the learners achieved literacy according to the NLM norm, the SCs and STs and backward classes were assessed to be 91.76 per cent, the campaign was able to mobilize excellent support from all sections of the district, the *Jagriti* centres and the village committees performed their responsibilities in an excellent manner to seek individual organisational and financial support for the programme, in their respective area of operation and the programme of environment building was very effective and was mainly based on wall writing, '*Kala Jatha* and local *Jatha's* performances, literacy functions, media support, video-film shows etc.

The Misra (1994) of Vikaram University evaluated the TLC in Ratlam (Madhya Pradesh) and found that

1. 86.46 per cent of the sample neo-literates reached the NLM norms of proficiency.
2. Among the various sectors, Jaora showed the highest results *i.e.*, 98.26 per cent followed by Ratlam Gramin Area, 91.10 per cent Alot, 89.06 per cent, Sailana 86.83 per cent and Jaura Gramin 83.93 per cent.
3. Distribution of neo-literates according to their total score shows that 45 per cent of the neo-literates obtained the score of above 80 followed by score of 70-79 by 31.27 per cent and only 13 per cent have obtained less than the score of 60.
4. Letter writing was the weakest point in neo-literates. Achievement in reading, writing and numeracy and oral questions were calculated as 92.03, 75.77, 70.27 and 79.06 per cent respectively.

5. Achievement of rural areas ranged from 69.53, to 91.19 per cent, while in urban area it ranged higher *i.e.*, 69.53 per cent to 98.26 per cent.

Mushtaq Ahmed (1994) evaluated the TLC of Agra. The findings of the study shows that :

1. 5613 out of 8,011 sample learners —achieved the NLM norms of literacy providing a success rate of 70.06 per cent.
2. Age group-wise performance 73.38 per cent in the age group 9–14, 69.67 per cent in 15–35 and 67.07 per cent in 35–40 achieved the NLM norms literacy.
3. Urban areas performed better with 75.30 per cent success in comparison to the rural area, the overall success rate of 70.06 per cent indicated the district had done well.

Mushtaq Ahmed (1994) evaluated the TLC in Almora and the findings of the study were as follows;

The learners' outcome of this district was 40.3 per cent on the NLM norms. Some villages deemed best by the ZSS, were also separately tested. Their outcome came to be only 38.1 per cent which was less than that of the whole district. Among the Blocks, the performance of Kapl had proved to be the best *i.e.* 49.3 per cent.

Studies on the JSNs

Vasumathi, T. (1992) studied the organization and functioning of *Jana Shikshana Nilayams* under Area Development Approach of the National Literacy Mission in the colleges of Kannur District. The objectives of the study were :

(1) To study the extent and nature of Jana *Shikshana Nilayams* (JSN),
(2) To find out the procedure in selecting the area for and location of JSNs,
(3) To estimate the present strength of neoliterates coming under the JSNs in each college,
(4) To find out the number of beneficiaries of JSNs,
(5) To assess the selection procedure of *preraks*,
(6) To find out the physical and learning facilities provided for the neo-literates and beneficiaries,

(7) To find out the details regarding sex, age, educational qualification, training etc. of the *preraks* and programme officers,

(8) To study the discharge of duties of the *preraks* and programme officers,

(9) To examine the extent of coverage of Scheduled Castes, Scheduled Tribes and women,

(10) To investigate about the cultural and co-curricular programmes organised by the JSNs,

(11) To investigate into the techniques of evaluation adopted,

(12) To find out the problems faced by the *preraks* and programme officers,

(13) To put forth recommendations on the basis of findings emerging out of the study.

Nair. Omana and Rahim (1992) studied the programmes and activities of JSN organised by Nehru Yuva Kendras in Kerala. The findings reveal that an equal number of men and women were involved as *preraks* and majority of *preraks* in the age group of 19-20 years with annual income ranges from 1000 to 2000 rupees. On the other hand, nearly half of the then belong to backward communities.

The study also discloses that majority of preraks had adequate experience in Total Literacy Campaign as instructors and master trainers, majority of the preraks were affiliated to some cultural or sports organisations and interest in social work promoted them to join as preraks.

With regard to physical facilities available, 1/3rd of the JSNs possessed improvised teaching. Half of them had a separate reading room but none of them were having own buildings. The major source for the books and the other material were found to e Nehru Yuva Kendras and all of them were receiving news papers. Dropouts and inadequate funds were the major problems of the JSNs.

Muthuchamy (1992) studied the role performance of the preraks and found that there is a discripancy between the ideal, and actual performance of *preraks* in the roles as organisers of Literacy/post-literacy activities (56.25%), generator of awareness (62.60%), organisers of' cultural and recreational programmes (56%), mobilisers of resources (60.64%) recorders of educational activities

(35.20%) professional devotion (61.20%) guidance activity (65.86%). and Supervisory functions (38.88%).

Adilakshmi (1993) investigated into the working conditions of the JSNs and found that the *preraks* organise JCKs confined to the post-literacy activities alone. None of the *Jana Shikshana Nilayams* were provided with audio-visual facilities. The study also revealed that there is no difference between the working conditions of JSN organised by the *preraks* among different age and experienced groups.

The State Resource Centre of Karnataka (1995) conducted an observational study to identify the role of JSN in continuing education with the objectives:

(1) To examine the functions of *prerak* and JSNs,
(2) to study the activities of JSNs in relation to literacy campaign and continuing education programmes.
(3) to study the listening efforts of the preraks and local public;
(4) to examine the utility of infrastructural facilities provided to the JSNs, and
(5) To identify the problems existing in and of the JSNs;

The findings of the study are as follows.

(1) Majority of the libraries of JSN were kept open from 8 AM to 10 AM and 4 PM to 6 PM and a few of them were open through out the day.
(2) The Educated visit JSN's to read news papers only. However, school going children/ school dropouts were the regular users of JSNs.
(3) Story books and thrillers were found to be popular.
(4) Inadequate availability of books on professionally related and vocation related or job related literature in JSN.
(5) Majority of the *preraks* lacked motivation, insight an vision for running JSN and failed to meet the demands of public in terms of needed information/ skills and training of the local youth.
(6) Although majority of the preraks were well qualified no evidence of success of JSNs in terms of furthering literacy and continuing education.

(7) No evidence and support for the claims of conducting cultural, sports, folk and other literary activities

(8) A large quantity of good quality reading materials were kept idle in JSNs.

(9) The facilities provided to the preraks viz. bicycle, sewing machines, the radio, two-in-ones were missing from JSN or misused by the *prerak*. The public reported that the material, musical instruments required chronic replacement or repair

(10) Only 5% of the JSNs were found to run effectively in one respect or the other

(11) Only 35 JSNs had their own buildings.

(12) The post literacy centres, the *Grama Shikshana Samithies* have become almost ineffective/disfunctional and a result the JSns have become handicapped.

(13) The *preraks* of the JSNs were under paid and their positions were insecure. There was inordinate delay and disorganisation in the payment

(14) The payment of contingent grants to all the functionaries of JSNs involved a great amount of cumbersome practice.

(15) There was a great deal of administrative and interdepartmental procedures involved in providing electricity in JSNs

(16) The problems of JSNs in the state were the non existence of own buildings for JSN's, theft, lack of place, remoteness etc.

(17) The JSNs have been ignored wilfully regarding their roles in JCKs or education for all. JSNs have no place nor responsibility in the network of this movement. As a result, they were neither obligated nor accountable to literacy movements.

Operation Research Group of DAE (1994) has evaluated the functioning of the scheme of JSNs for highlighting its strengths and weaknesses and to provide certain recommendations to overcome the existing deficiences. The major findings of the study are as follows.

1. Overall Impact.

The continuing Education Programme, on the whole, has had a positive impact on the rural population. The provision of JSN facilities has succeeded in enhancing the demand for education, particularly continuing education, which is apparent from high participation levels.

The need for grass root level institute catering to continuing education is being acutely felt in post TLC districts.

2. Participation in JSN activities

a. *Library* - The library is found to be the most popular activity of the JSN and is used by people from all age groups. There is a strong demand for a more versatile library facility and for adoption of a decentralised process of selection of reading materials. There were more books available to cater to the formally educated than the neo-literates.

b. Sports, Recreational and Cultural Activities—Sports was observed to be the second most popular activity of the JSN. Availability of sports equipments and musical instruments had served the purpose of making the JSN more attractive to the rural people. However, in most JSNs, condition of sports materials was found to be bad.

c. *Literacy classes* - Holding of evening classes is perceived to be an important function of the *Preraks* by the community and a majority of the *Preraks* did organise such classes. Largest share of evening class attenders were semi-literates from AE programmes.

d. *Discussion groups* - The central level of awareness among the learners' groups regarding charcha Mandals organised through JSNs was observed 'to be very' low. Charcha Mandals catered mostly to exclusive male groups and there is not much participation by women largely because of the conservative social norms and the dual responsibilities which they have to perform at home and in the field.

e. *Training programmes;* Organizing training programmes has been found to be the most neglected activity of the JSNs. Less than 20% of the *Preraks* reported to have organised any such activity. Also, JSNs were hardly used by other Govt. Departments to impart training or knowledge regarding various schemes or any other developmental issues.

3. Catering Capacity of JSNs.

The norm of having one JSN per 5,000 population was found to be too optimistic. In practice, each JSN caters to less than 250 people. For hilly States like Mozoram, the concept of having one JSN to cover

4-5 villages leads to inaccessibility which clearly indicates that separate set of norms will have to be evolved for allocating JSNs in different regions.

4. Infrastructural/Resource Support.

a. No budget has been provided for training of Preraks and in most of the States, the Preraks developed to run the JSNs have not received any training at all. Selection of the Preraks in many of the States has not been made in accordance with the prescribed criteria. In places where village Education Committees were associated in the selection process, the Preraks chosen were found to be more acceptable to the community.

b. Shortage of manpower and infrastructure available to the District Adult Education Officers (DAEOs) have adversely affected the supervision and monitoring of the programme. No specific budgetary provisions have been made in the programme to cover expenses on supervision and monitoring. After the withdrawal of RELP, no formal posts of Project Officers or Assistant Project Officers exist to provide an organizational structure for the management of the JSNs. This lack of manpower and absence of adequate interaction between the DAEOs and the Preraks have adversely affected the programme performance.

c. Delays in payment of honorarium to Preraks have effectively reduced the commitment level leading even to closure of JSN, insufficient amount of honorarium is also perceived to be one of the major reasons for non- performance of Preraks. Crucial out of pocket expenses traveling and postage costs are not reimbursed through the programme, which has further hampered the performance of the JSNs.

d. In most states, the expectation of donation of a space by the community to run the JSN have not been realised. The current JSN programme does not have a budget provision for reimbursing the amount paid for rented accommodation. Quite often, preraks have been forced to run the JSNs from their own residence which has drastically hindered community participations.

Reddeppa (1993) studied the Determinants of prerak Effectiveness. The aim of the study is to measure the effectiveness of the Preraks, relationship between prerak effectiveness and their characteristics and to find out the differences between prerak effectiveness. Scores obtained by the preraks belonging to different groups.

The findings of the study are as follows:

1. The preraks selected for organisation of JSNs are men from unprivileged sections, belong to agricultural background from lower income groups with less education, less experience, married and belong to younger age group.
2. Association between prerak characteristics and effectiveness reveals that the association between and effectiveness is significant from all sources of ratings. Further sex and effectiveness is also significantly associated as per learners rating point of view.
3. There is no significant difference between men and women preraks in their effectiveness. However, the effectiveness scores shows that women preraks were found to be more effective.
4. Preraks belonging to forward caste were found to be more effective followed by BC group.
5. Preraks with agricultural background were found to be more effective than other groups.
6. Preraks with more income were found to be more effective than lower income groups.
7. Preraks with more education were found to be more effective.
8. Married preraks were found to be more effective than unmarried preraks.
9. Preraks in the higher age groups were found to be more effective than younger preraks.
10. Preraks with more positive aptitude were found to be more effective than those with less positive aptitude.

Problems of the Post-Literacy Workers

Muthuchamy (1992) identified the problems of the preraks in performing the roles prescribed for the preraks. The problems of the preraks in organising JSNs., Lack of interest among the people for learning, lack of effective planning, inadequate physical facilities and proper place for JSN, Non availability graded materials, lack of sufficient training for the *preraks*, limited knowledge possessed by the preraks, inadequate supply of neo-literate materials, lack of motivation on the part of learners, lack of transport facilities, inadequate audio-visual aids, difficulty in bringing the experts to the villages, inability of the prerak in contacting the specialists, non-availability of the local talents; non existence of Mahila Mandals and youth clubs, lack of measuring instruments of functionality and awareness among the adults, lack of technical/professional skills, inadequate training, personal and social problems of the preraks.

In addition to the above, the study also found that women preraks over 30 years other than these of S.Cs. better qualified, more experienced were found to be the best role performers.

Kumaraswamy, T. and Padmanabhaiah (1995) identified the problems faced by the monitors at the grass root level and found out the solutions. The specific objectives are as follows.

1. To find out the problems faced by monitors in organising JCKs.
2. To find out whether there exists only significant difference between men and women monitors in perceiving the problems.
3. To suggest measures to overcome the problems.

The findings of the study are as follows:

1. Out of 32 problems perceived by monitors, problems 1-20 (checked by majority of the sample which means significantly more severe problems) and 30-32 (checked by about one-third of the sample which means significantly more severe problems) and 30-32 (checked by about one-third of the sample which means significantly less severe problems) are found to be statistically significant at 0.05 level. Problems 21–29 are moderately severe problems and around half of the sample have checked them and the chi-square value of these items was not significant. Out of the above problems priority has to be given to solve the problems 1–20. A glance at these problems denotes the problems 1–3 are related to physical facilities, 4-8 and 14-18 are related to administrative matters, 9 and 10 are related to learners whereas problems 11–13, 19 and 20 are related to community report.

2. With regard to gender difference in perceiving the problems men and women monitors of the sample differed significantly on problems 1,6, 8, 13, 14 22, 24 and 30. Among these, the problems 1, 6 and 14 significantly were more common to men and the remaining 5 problems more severe to women. The nature of the problems more severe to men and women indicates that men monitors require more freedom and control over the programme and women monitors need more involvement of other functioneries.

In addition to above the investigations also suggested certain measures to overcome the problems faced by the monitors.

From the above review, it is clear that the studies conducted in the area of adult education and the JSN in particular are very few and need more attention. In view of the fast expansion of the total literacy campaign approach more and more post-literacy programme infrastructure has been created and which needs more efficient human resources to handle the same for successful implementation of the programme.

The review of the above studies clearly demonstrates that not many studies have been conducted to identify the problems of the field functionaries especially the monitors working in P.L.Cs. Hence, the present study has taken up to identify the problems of the monitors and to prepare a list of anticipated problems of the monitors so as to help the existing monitors to equip themselves and would be monitors by evolving training, curriculum and to evolve suitable strategies to overcome the same.

3

STATEMENT OF THE PROBLEM

This chapter deals with the statement of the problem which consists of the title of the study, definitions of certain terms used in the study, objectives, hypotheses, scope of the study, need and importance and limitations of the study.

Title of the Study

" An Enquiry into the Problem Faced by the Monitors In Jana Chaithanya Kendras".

Objectives of the Study

The objectives of the study are:

1. To identify the problems of monitors in organising the JCKs.
2. To findout the relationship between the personal traits and problems of the monitors.
3. To find out the differences if any, in the intensity of the problems faced by the Monitors due to variations in their sex, caste, occupation, income, experience, education and marital status.

Hypothesis of the Study

Based on the objectives, the following hypotheses were formulated for testing.

1. There is no significant association between the personal traits (sex, caste, occupation, income, experience, education and marital status) and the problems faced by the JCK monitors.
2. There is no significant difference in each problem and problems as a whole faced by JCK monitors under the area 'Organisation' of JCK activities due to variations in their sex, caste, occupation, income, experience, educational status and marital status.
3. There is no significant problem and problems as a whole faced by JCK monitors under the area 'Administration' of JCK activities due to variations in their sex, caste, occupation, income, experience, educational status and marital status.
4. There is no significant difference in each problem and problems as a whole faced by JCK monitors under the area 'Environment', of JCK activities due to variations in their sex, caste, occupation, income, experience, educational status and marital status.
5. There is no significant difference in each problem and problem as a whole faced by JCK monitors under the area 'Co-operation' of JCK activities due to variations in their sex, caste, occupation, income, experience, educational status and marital status.
6. There is no significant difference in each problem and problems as a whole faced by JCK monitors under the area 'Material', of JCK activities due to variations in their sex, caste, occupation, income, experience, educational status and marital status.

Scope of the Study

The success of the literacy programmes to a greater extent depends on the follow-up activities done after the literacy programmes. This is more true with respect to T.L.Cs. Realising this, greater emphasis is given for post-literacy porgrammes in T.L.Cs. In Chittoor district also as a part of Total Literacy Programme, provision was made for post-literacy activities in the form of JCKs. These JCKs are expected to conduct varied activities and each JCK is managed by a monitor chosen from local community having adequate experience in literacy activities.

In discharging several activities of JCKs, the monitors may come across several problems. The problems may be related to organisation, administration and academic, environment building and problems related to human as well as material resources. The present study aimed at studying the problems of the monitors of the JCKs with special reference to organisational, administrative and academic, environment, mobilisation of human and material resources. It also focuses attention to see the association between personal variables of the monitors and their problems in the organisation of JCK activities. Further, the attention is also paid towards identifying the significant differences if any, in the intensity of the problems faced by the monitors due to variations in their sex, caste, occupation, income, experience, educational status and marital status.

Need and Importance of the Study

The planning for post-literacy and continuing education in Chittoor District of Andhra Pradesh was chalked out by the ZSS well before the campaign in order to ensure continuity in the programme and to prevent the neo-literates from relapsing into illiteracy. At present, the campaign is in its fifth year. The post-literacy Centres in Chittoor District are known as " Jana Chaithanya Kendras" (JCKs) and more than ten thousand JCKs are functioning throughout the district. The volunteers who worked with dedication and commitment during the literacy phase were appointed as Monitors.

The functions of monitors are wide and varied starting from organising post-literacy Centres to develop enlightened citizens, with a better standard of living. The Monitor has to strive to promote reading, writing and computational skills among the learners. He has to decide the timings of the Centres in consultation with the learners to compensate the loss of learning. He should provide information to various occupational groups to improve their personal sill. The Monitor has to organise *Churcha Mandals* to generate " awareness" among the community with regard to the problems and overcome the same through collective action. The Monitor should arrange useful lectures by experts in various fields and use local talent for the promotion of functional skills among the neo-literates. He should involve the education youth and enlist support of *Mahila Mandals* and youth Clubs in running the Centre. It is important to organise the post-literacy Centres in the best direction possible by adopting several strategies from time to time to overcome the problems in organising the JCKs.

The success of JCKs. largely lies on the capacity and capabilities of the Monitor in overcoming the local problems and in adopting the local environment. Further, Monitors should be in a position to identify the problems and to formulate suitable strategies to overcome them in the process of achieving the objectives of the JCKs. However, not all the Monitors were in a position to do the above due to their varied socio-economic and educational backgrounds. Hence in order to improve the efficiency of the Monitor in particular and the programme as a whole, it is necessary to identify the common problems of the working Monitors so as to equip them through pre-service training which inturn facilitate so as to formulate suitable strategies depending on the nature and extent of the problems to overcome them. Keeping in view the above, the present study on the identification of the problems of the monitors were formulated.

Limitations of the Study

1. The present study is limited to the monitors working in Chittoor District of Rayalaseema Region in Andhra Pradesh State.
2. The study is limited to find out the problems of the Monitors only in organising JCKs.
3. The personal factors of the Monitors such as Sex, caste, occupation, income, experience, education and marital status are only chosen for analysing their association with the problems.
4. The study has involved only 200 Monitors.
5. To identify the problems and their intensity, the rating scale is the only tool used.

4

METHOD OF INVESTIGATION

This chapter deals with the methodology followed in the study, the procedure adopted in the construction of the tool, locale of the study, sample of the study, method of collecting data and the statistical procedures adopted in the study.

Construction of the Tools

Selection of the tool

The aim of the study is to identify the problems of the monitors in organising various activities of JCKs functioning under ZSS of Chittoor District and to find out the relationship between the problems and the personal traits of the Monitors.

In order to identify the problems of the monitors and to study their relationship with their personal traits, a problem inventory is required. As the review of literature clearly shows there is no readily available specific tool for measuring the problems of the monitors or there is no relevant tool which can be adopted for the purpose of the present study. Hence, the problem inventory to measure the problems of the monitors *viz.*

JCKs Monitors' Problem Inventory' (JCKMPI) is developed by the investigator.

Inadequate availability of the books relevant to the interest of the learners, Lack of recognition to the monitors on par with social workers, JCKs' inability to provide training in suitable occupational skills to the women, Inadequate training for the Monitors for effective implementation of JCK, Reinduction of drop-outs into the schools, Obtaining co-operation from experts and officials of developmental departments –these items come under co-operational problems.

Getting return of the books from borrowers, Lack of training and experience among the Monitors for conducting cultural programmes, Lack of suitable place for organisation of Sports and Games, Lack of regular supply of Newspapers to JCK, Lack of motivation among Communities to participate in *Charcha Mandals*, Organisation of activities in all affiliated hamlets of the JCK, Lack of adequate lighting facilities in JCK, Organising need based activities in the JCK–these items belong to Material problems.

Description of the Tool used

The monitors' problems can be identified and studied by adopting various methods and sources. The problems can be identified by using various methods such as interview, observation, checklist, questionnaire, ratings etc. The sources of identification of the problems can be personal interview with the monitors, observation of actual proceedings of the JCK, enquiry with the field administrators etc.

Each of the above methods and sources have their own merits and demerits. However, for the purpose of the present study, the rating scale method will be the appropriate method for not only identifying the problems but also to study their intensity with regard to the sources, the monitors themselves will be the appropriate source for identification of the problems. Hence for the purpose of study, the rating scale method was used by which one can identify the problem as well as their intensity. Further, this method helps in categorising the problems based on their intensity expressed by the monitors.

i) Advantages of The Rating Scales:

The advantages of the rating scale are as follows.

1. Rating requires much less time than the ranking method.

2. The procedure becomes interesting when graphic method is employed.
3. That can be used with persons having minimum of training for making ratings.
4. The range of its application is very wide. It can be used for teaching ratings, personality ratings, testing validity or paper pencil inventories, school appraisal etc.

ii) Types of rating scale:

1. Numerical scale
2. Graphic scale
3. Descriptive scale
4. Cumulative scale
5. Standard scale.

1. *Numerical Scale* : In a five-point scale, for example, the 'average' person scored 0, the deviants scored +2, +1, –2 or –1, or the scores to eliminate signs can all be positive, 1 being the lowest, 3 the average, 5 the highest. For example, how was the lesson introduced in the class?

No.	*Trait*
1.	Very Unsatisfactory
2.	Unsatisfactory
3.	Satisfactory
4.	Good
5.	Outstanding

2. *Graphic Scale* : A common variant of the scoring method is the graphic rating scale. The several levels, or degrees of the trait are defined and placed at points along a horizontal line. The judge places a mark anywhere he chooses on this line between the two extremes. Although a graphic scale theoretically permits scoring a large number of points, such refinement and spurious accuracy are not warranted. This may be expressed as under:

Trait responsibility for completing work:

Very high High Average Low Very low

3. *Descriptive scale* : The rater puts a check (/) in the blank before the trait which is described in a word or phrase.

Ex : Do the people take the initiative?
- show marked originality
- willing to take initiative
- quite inventive
- on the whole unenterprising
- very dependent on others.

4. *Cumulative Points Scale*: An individual rates himself. He checks his traits on a list of objectives. He then counts his favourable and unfavourable responses. For each item, there are two responses to be weighed as +1 and 0.
5. *Standard Scale* : A set of standard is presented to the ratings. Ratings through this scale become easier and more meaningful. For example, man to man ratings, hand writing comparison.

Development of the tool

A list of monitor problems were gathered from different sources like personal interviews with the monitors, village co-ordinators, participants of the programme, based on consultation with the experts in the field and the review of related literature. The items pooled were again rewritten by removing the ambiguous items, items without clarity, repetition and inaccuracies. These items were arranged under different sub-headings. The list thus prepared was presented to a panel of 5 experts and suggestions of the experts were carried out. At this stage, there were 65 items in the inventory.

The JCK Monitor Problem Inventory consists of two sections. The section one of the inventory deals with the data pertaining to the monitors background such as *viz.* sex, caste, occupation, income, experience, education and marital status, Section two deals with the monitors problems in the implementation of various activities of the JCK.

Rating Procedure

Keeping in view of the background of the sample and opinion of the experts in the field, it was thought that the rating chosen should be as simple as possible to facilitate the sample to indicate the rating with ease and accuracy. The five-point numerical rating scale consisting of five descriptive cues *viz.*, fully agree, agree, undecided, disagree and fully disagree having the scores 5,4,3,2 and 1 respectively. The respondents were supposed to agree with any of the alternative cues to indicate the intensity of the problems they are facing.

Pilot Study

The purpose of the present study is to identify the problems of the monitors. Hence, the appropriate sample for pilot study were the monitors. A sample of 100 monitors were selected at random fm different Jana Chaitanya Kendras in Chittoor District of Andhra Pradesh. However, care was taken to see that the sample selected should represent all sections of the society. Before administration of the scale, the purpose and mode of filling the scale was explained to the monitors for gathering the accurate data.

Selection of Items

Based on the JCK Monitor Problems inventory scores, the JCK Monitor Problem Inventories were arranged in decending order. The top 27 JCK Monitor Problem Inventories (27 per cent) were chosen to find out the discriminative power and usefulness of the items chosen for the Inventory. The 't' values for each of the items were calculated as per the procedure suggested by Edward (1969). Items that had calcualted 't' value equal or greater than 1.75 were selected for inclusion in the final from and all those items with 't' values less than 1.75 were discarded. Based on this procedure, 17 items were discarded and final form of the inventory consisted of 38 problems.

At this stage 10 items were under organisation problems, 8 items in Administration problems, 6 items in Environment problem, 6 items in Co-operation problems and 8 items in Material problems.

Reliability of the tool

There are several methods to estimate the reliability of the scale. Some of the commonly used methods for finding out the reliability of the scale were:

1. Test, re-test reliability

2. Split-half reliability
3. Alternate (or) Parallel form reliability
4. Kutar-Richardson Estimates

For the purpose of the present study, Test, re-test reliability of the scale was adopted. This was done by obtaining the ratings for the scale twice with an interval of one month between the first and second administration of the scale to the sample. The obtained correlation coefficient between the two ratings was 0.02 which is significant. Therefore, the JCK Monitor problem Inventory used in the study is a highly reliable one.

Validity of the Tool

Any instrument developed for measuring a particular aspect will be considered appropriate only when its validity is proved. Construct validity refers to the extent to which a test reflects constructs persumed to underline the test performance and also the extent to which it is based on theories regarding these constructs. The JCK Monitor Problem Inventory developed on the lines described above possesses satisfactory validity with reference to the content, items and instrinsic validity. The description of details relating to the validity of the Inventory was as follows.

i) *Content Validity:* Content validity indicates how adequately is the content of a test-sampling, the domain about which inferences are to be made. Further, when taken collectively, the items should constitute a representative sample of the variable that is measured. The present JCK Monitor Problem Inventory was developed keeping the above in view i.e., while selecting the items the functionaries of the programme, researchers and review of literature was consulted. Thus, it can be reasonably assumed that the instrument possesses satisfactory content validity.

ii) *Items Validity* : Item validity stresses the extent to which the item predicts segregation of examines into those with high versus those with low criterion scores. The discriminative power of each of the items of the present scale was established by calculating their 't' values as described under the heading 'Selection of items'. Thus, the items chosen for both parts of the scale were found to be effectively valid.

iii) *Intrinsic Validity*: Intrinsic validity indicate the degree to which a test measures what it purports to measure. This can also be stated as how will the obtained scores measure the tests, true score component. Intrinsic validity refers to the Square root of its reliability. Thus, the intrinsic validity of the JCK Monitor Problems Inventory was the square root of its reliability 0.92= 0.959 which can be assumed that the scores have highly satisfying intrinsic validity.

Sample of Design

The locale of the study was the Chittoor District of Andhra Pradesh. There are 10,000 JCKs functioning under the ZSS in 66 Mandals of 3 Revenue Divisions *i.e.*, Tirupati was selected randomly at the first stage of the sample selection. In the second stage, out of the total monitors working in the division, 200 monitors were chosen at random as the sample of the study.

DATA Collection

To get the required data, the researcher has met all the Mandal Development officers and Mandal co-ordinators of the Total Literacy Programme and explained about the aim of the study and requested for their permission. They gave permission and co-operation for collecting the information required for the study.

The investigator visited all the selected JCKs and administered the JCK Monitor Problem Inventory to the monitors and also explained the mode of filling the same.

Statistical Techniques Used in the Study

The data, thus gathered were pooled together and analysed keeping in view the objectives of the study in mind. The statistical techniques like - Mean, SD, Chisquare, 't' test and ANOVA were applied to draw the inferences. Further, an attempt was also made to categories the problems into Prominent, Moderate and Less Prominent problems based on the intensity of the problem checked by the sample.

5

RESULTS AND DISCUSSION

Monitor is the actual doer of adult education at the community level through various activities of the JCKs. The efficiency of the monitor largely lies in effective performance of the assigned roles to him. In the process of discharging his/her roles he/she has to face lot of problems as the clientele to be covered by him. In the process of discharging his/her roles he/she has to face lot of problems as the clientele to be covered by him were of from different backgrounds. The quality of his performance will be very high if the monitor is able to overcome the problems through tact and intelligence. This capacity to overcome the problems can be enhanced by having adequate knowledge of anticipated problems of monitors in the field situation. Keeping the above in view, the present investigation was formulated with the following objectives.

1. To identify the problems of monitors in organising the JCKs.
2. To findout the relationship between the personal traits (Sex, Caste, Occupation, Income, Experience, Educational status and Marital status) and the problems of the monitors.
3. To findout the differences if any, in the intensity of the problems faced by the Monitors due to variations in their Sex, Caste, Occupation, Income, Experience, Educational status and Marital status.

Keeping the above objectives in view the results of the study are presented in three sections. Section-1 of the study deals with the categorisation of the problem items of the monitors into Prominent problems, Moderate problems and Less Prominent Problems. In section–II, the association between the selected characteristics of monitor and problems of the monitors were studied as a whole and areaways. The relationship between the selected characteristics of the monitors and the problem were studied both in terms of area-wise and itemwise in section–III of the study.

SECTION 1

Classification of the problems of the Monitors

In order to highlight the important problems of the monitors in discharging their duties/roles, the problems were classified into three groups based on the intensity of the problems checked by the monitors. The criteria of mean ± ½ S.D was used to classify the items. As per the above criteria, the problem items with mean value of 3.49 and above were treated as prominent problems of the monitors, and items with mean value of 3.12 and less were treated as less prominent problems. The items with mean values falling between 3.49 and 3.12 were treated as moderate problems of the monitors. Based on this, out of 38 items 12 items were found to be Prominent problems, 13 items Moderate and rest 13 Less Prominent. From the above it appears that nearly one third of the identified items were found to be Prominent problems affecting the performance of the monitors in other words the quality of the programme.

The classified problems *viz.* the prominent the moderate and the less prominent were presented in the following tables.

Prominent Problems of the Monitors in the organisation of JCK Activities

Table 1 discloses that out of 38 items 12 items are found to be very prominent problems for the monitors in organising various activities of the programme.

Table 1: Mean and Standard Deviation of the Problems faced by the monitors under the category of prominent problems in the organisation of JCK activities.

S.No.	Nature of the Problem	Mean	S.D.
1.	Lack of Provision for honorarium to the Monitors.	3.98	1.43
2.	Lack of suitable co-operation from development departments officials for the implementation of the decisions of the Charcha Mandals.	3.93	1.18
3.	Lack of suitable sports and games materials at the JCK	3.92	1.34
4.	Borrowing of good number of books by educated leaving little scope for neo-literates.	3.84	1.38
5.	Lack of Audio-Visual aids to disseminate the information to the learners in JCK.	3.82	1.35
6.	Lack of recognition to the monitors on par with social workers.	3.81	1.49
7.	JCKs' inability to provide training in suitable occupational skills to women due to lack of co-operation from developmental departments.	3.73	1.36
8.	Lack of provision for the production of posters and charts for the propagation of JCK activities.	3.66	1.47
9.	Lack of suitable literacy materials for the promotion of literacy.	3.61	1.41
10.	Lack of information on developmental programme.	3.58	1.25
11.	Lack of effective co-operation from the village leaders for implementation of the decisions of the Charcha Mandals.	3.50	1.47
12.	Irrelevancy of the available books in JCK to the interest of adults.	3.49	1.37

The above table also reveals that most of the prominent problems are related to the materials that are available and which are not available, co-operation from Villagers and Officials, ability in providing occupational skills and finally they concerned about their status and honorarium. From the above it appears that not at all the JCKs were equipped to cater to the needs of the people. Hence it is suggested that programmers should take note of this and should provide suitable and relevant books, sports materials, Audio visual aids, posters, charts, information on developmental programmes, on urgent basis to all JCKs. The officials concerned with development departments should be advised to co-operate with the activities of the JCKs so that the developmental information will reach the target without much effort. Further, the services of the monitors should also be recognised on par with other social workers both in terms of social as well as financial status.

Moderate Problems of the Monitors in the Organisation of JCK Activities

Table– 2 reveals that out of 38 problems, 13 items were identified as Moderate problems of the monitors. Though these problems were identified as moderate problems the obtained mean value of the items indicates that they were also checked by a large number of monitors.

Table 2: Mean and Standard Deviation of the problems faced by the monitors under the category of moderate problems in the organisation of JCK activities.

S.No.	Nature of the Problem	Mean	S. D.
1.	Getting return of the books from borrowers.	3.47	1.35
2.	Lack of training and suitable materials to the monitors for conducting cultural programmes.	3.43	1.53
3.	Lack of suitable infrastructure for the organisation of sports and games.	3.34	1.40
4.	Irregular supply of news papers to JCK.	3.33	1.50
5.	Lack of suitable materials to motivate the communities participate in the Charcha Mandals.	3.32	1.26
6.	Lack of adequate facilities in the organisation of activities in all affiliated hamlets of the JCK.	3.26	1.55
7.	Lack of adequate lighting facilities in JCK.	3.23	1.58
8.	Inability in providing different occupational skills to neo-literates.	3.22	1.28
9.	The traditional beliefs and customs are becoming obstacles in organising activities relating to women empowerment.	3.21	1.49
10.	Inadequate training to the monitors for effective implementation of JCK activities in co-operation with local experts.	3.16	1.29
11.	Ability to maintain hormonious relationship with the villagers.	3.13	1.15
12.	Lack of equal participation on the part of men and women in activities of JCK	3.13	1.39
13.	Lack of co-operation from the school for reinduction of dropouts children.	3.12	1.37

The identified problems under this category shows that the problems are of different kinds and covers almost all the areas of activities of the JCK. The Moderate problems relates to the lack of adequate infrastructure, training, participation, co-operation from different sources for effective functioning of the JCKs. Hence, it is advised that suitable environment may be created by organising various activities leading to the creation of better awareness about the utility of literacy in their day to day life. Further, all the monitors may be retrained so as to enable them to organise simple occupational skill development programmes, for the benefit of the adults. The monitors should be equipped to motivate the target group and elicit their effective participation in all the activities of JCKs.

Less Prominent problems of the Monitors in the Organisation of JCK activities:

Table–3 present the items considered as less prominent problems by the monitors.

Monitors of JCKs found that these are not affecting their performance as monitors. Out of 38 items, 13 belong to this category. These items related to the material available, activities of the JCKs, co-operation from village leaders, experts and officials from developmental departments, motivating neo-literates for continuing education village level literacy committees. Village politics and capabilities of monitors etc. were found to be Less Prominent problems in organising various activities of JCKs. However, the obtained mean value of the items were found to be more than 2.50. It appears these are also prominent for some of the monitors. Hence it is suggested that the programme implementors should also concentrate on these items for improvement of the quality of the programme.

Table -3 : Mean and Standard Deviation of the problems faced by the monitors under the category of less prominent problems in the organisation of JCK activities.

S.No.	Nature of the Problem	Mean	S.D.
1.	Lack of suitable materials in organising need based activities.	3.09	1.20
2.	Obtaining co-operation from experts and officials and developmental departments.	3.03	1.41
3.	The standard of language in the available reading materials in JCK is higher than the learners' standard.	3.03	1.31
4.	Charcha Mandal activities were affected due to village politics.	3.03	1.42
5.	Taking special care of the backward learners.	2.99	1.37
6.	Electitation of co-operation from the village leaders.	2.97	1.28
7.	Accommodating representatives of various groups in village level literate committee.	2.93	1.51
8.	Ability to motivate the neo-literates for continuing education.	2.91	1.99
9.	Choosing a suitable place for effective learning.	2.88	1.24
10.	The working monitors' age and experience does not suit for discussion of village problems in Charcha Mandals.	2.88	1.27
11.	Involvement of village politics in organising JCK activities.	2.81	1.48
12.	The JCK activities were affected by different castes and religions.	2.80	1.52
13.	Lack of skills among the monitors for identifying learning problems among the adults in acquisition of literacy.	2.74	1.49

SECTION –II

Association Between Personal Characteristics Of the Monitor and Problem Areas

In order to study the association between personal characteristics of the monitors and the problems encountered by them, the monitors were also categorised into three groups *viz.* Monitors having Prominent Problems, Moderate Problems and Less prominent Problems.

The obtained chi-square between different groups of monitors categorised according to their characteristics and in relation to different areas of the problems are presented in Table –4.

The results presented in Table–4 clearly reveals the following:.

The association between the caste and problems relating to the organisation and co-operation were found to be significantly associated and the association between characteristics and rest of the areas were found to be not significant. Hence the formulated hypothesis, " There is no significant association between the personal traits and the problems faced by the JCK Monitor" is accepted with respect to Caste in relation to the areas organisation and co-operation only.

The table clearly reveal that the other personal characteristics such as Sex, Occupation, Income, Experience, Educational status and Marital status in relation to the Monitors in different problem areas of the study are not associated and significant. Hence, the stated hypothesis is rejected with respect to the above variables.

Table –4: List of the variables problems areas and their respective chi-square values.

Problem areas	Organisation	Administration	Environment	Co-operative	Marital
Characteristics					
Sex	2.88@	2.13@	3.99@	1.91@	1.10@
Caste	12.53*	8.67@	6.62@	9.87*	3.39@
Occupation	6.22@	4.31@	6.11@	5.01@	3.61@
Income	1.32@	4.65@	7.47@	1.67@	7.03@
Experience	2.45@	1.82@	3.01@	1.68@	1.69@
Education	3.51@	2.11@	4.19@	3.08@	5.69@
Marital status	1.64@	0.06@	0.31@	4.65@	0.94@

Note : * Significant at 0.05 level
@ Not Significant at 0.05 level

SECTION —III

Influence of the Characteristics of the Monitors On their Problems

The influence of the characteristics of the monitors on their problems both areawise and itemwise were analysed and presented in this section. The results of the analysis were presented in three phases. In phase –I, the influence of the background of characteristics of monitors on their problems as a whole are discussed. In phase -II, the influence of characteristics on their problems in terms of areas are analysed. In Phase–III, the relation between the characteristics and individual problems are studied and presented.

Influence of Selected Characteristics of the Monitors on their Problems in the Area of Organisation of the JCK

The influence of the personal characteristics of the monitors *viz.* Sex, Caste, Occupation, Income, Experience, Education and Marital status on their problems in the area of organisation as a whole and individual items were studied, analysed, interpreted and presented in the following pages. Further, the prominent problems associated with different characteristics were also identified.

There are ten items in the area of organisation of JCKs. Based on the intensity of the problems checked by the monitors, the items were categorised into three groups based on the criteria of area men ± ½ S.D. as prominent problems, moderate problems and less prominent problem in the areas. The items, availability of not so relevant books at JCK, elecitation of co-operation from village leaders, village politics, lack of skills among the monitors for identification of learning problems among adults were fond to be moderate problems in the area. In view of the above it is necessary to supply only those books which were found to be relevant to needs and interest of the adult learners. Further awareness may be created among the community about the ill effects of the practice of the caste system and politicisation of the activities of the JCK. The monitors may also be trained in various activities relating to the process, acquisition of literacy and the factors associated, so as to enable them to identify the learning problems, backward learners and to take remedial steps to rectify them for enhancing the quality of the programme.

Further analysis was also made to identify the influence of the selected variable of the monitors on their problems by classifying the monitors into different groups based on their characteristics. The mean problem scores of the area as a whole and also itemwise were calculated between different groups and presented in the following tables.

The mean problems scores, S.Ds. and t/F values obtained by different groups of the monitors in the area of organisation were presented in the table.

Influence of the Sex on the Problems of the JCK Monitors in the Area of Organisation

From the Table-5 it appears that men and women monitors do not differ significantly with regard to their problems in the area of organisation. The obtained 't' value (0.650) is not significant at 0.05 level, However, the calculated mean problem scores discloses that men monitors has scored more mean value than women monitors. In other words, women monitors were found to be facing less problems than men in the area of organisation of JCK activities. In view of the above, further analysis was carried out to identify whether there were any items in this area associated with any of the sex group.

The results presented in the table demonstrate that men and women monitors differ significantly from each other on only one item *viz.* elecitation of co-operation from village leaders (± value : 2.23). In the Table–5 the mean and S.D. scores on each problem of JCK monitors under the area of organisation are presented.

Further the obtained mean problem scores reveal that men were not able to elecit more co-operation from villagers in JCK activities. However, the women felt that it is comparatively easier for them than for men to elicit co-operation from villagers in organising the JCK activities.

From the above it is concluded that sex has not significantly influenced the monitors' problems as a whole in the area of organisation of the JCK activities, whereas it has influenced the problem 'Elicitation of co-operation from villagers in JCK. Further, women are elciting better co-operation from villagers than men monitors.

Hence the hypothesis there is no significant difference in ecah problem and problems as a whole faced by JCK monitors under the area of organisation of JCK activities due to variation in their sex is rejected with respect to the problem no.7 of the table only.

In the remaining items in this area the obtained t' values were not significant. In other words the problems of men and women monitors were found to be similar in the area.

Influence of Caste on the Problems of the JCK Monitors in the Area of Organisation

In table 6 the mean and S.D. score of different groups of JCK Monitors on each problem and problem as a whole are presented in Table–6.

Table 6 reveals that the monitors belonging to SC/ST, B.C. groups does not differ significantly from each other with regard to the problems in organisation of JCKs. However, the obtained problems in organisation of JCKs. However, the obtained problem scores reveal that monitors belonging to backward caste groups felt easy in organising JCK than the other two groups felt easy in organising JCK than the other two groups viz forward caste and ST/STs which viewed the above problem similarly. In view of this further analysis was also made to identify the differences if any among these three groups on different items.

The itemwise analysis presented in Table–6 discloses that the monitors belonging to three caste groups does not differ on any of the items. In otherwords, all the three groups of monitors have experienced the problems in a similar manner. Hence the hypothesis " There is no significant difference in each problem and problems as a whole faced by JCK monitor under the area Organisation of JCK activities due to variations in their caste is accepted".

Table 5: Mean and Standard Deviation Problem Scores of both the sex group of JCK Monitors on each Item under the Area of 'Organisation' and the calculated 't' values.

Sl. No.	Nature of the problem	Men (N=60)		Women (N=60)		Calculated 't' values
		Mean	S.D	Mean	S.D.	
1.	Lack of provision for honorarium to the monitors.	2.93	1.25	2.82	1.22	0.56@
2.	Lack of suitable co-operation from developmental department officials for the implementation of the decisions of the Charcha Mandals.	3.22	1.29	2.97	1.09	1.14@
3.	Lack of provision for the production of posters and charts for the propagation of JCK activities.	3.22	1.40	3.02	1.32	0.80@
4.	Lack of suitable literacy materials for the promotion of literacy.	3.02	1.18	2.80	1.19	1.00@
5.	Lack of effective co-operation from the village leaders for implementation of the decisions of the Charcha Mandals.	3.13	1.47	2.85	1.25	1.15@
6.	Irrelevance of the available books in JCK to the interest of adults.	3.28	1.23	3.17	1.33	0.50@
7.	Elicitation of co-operation from the village leaders.	3.55	1.52	2.92	1.58	2.23*
8.	Involvement of village politics in organising JCK activities.	3.48	1.32	3.47	1.38	0.07@
9.	The JCK activities were affected by different castes and religions.	3.62	1.56	4.07	1.14	1.81@
10.	Lack of skills among the monitors for identifying of learning problems among the adults in aquisition of literacy.	3.00	1.64	3.52	1.40	1.86@
Problems as a whole		31.83	5.92	31.22	4.35	0.65@

Note : * Significant at 0.05 level
@ Not significant at 0.05 level

Table –6 : Mean and Standard Deviation Problem Scores of different caste groups of JCK Monitors on each Item under the Area of 'organisation' and the calculated 'f' values.

Sl.No.	Nature of the Problem	Caste						Calculated 'f' values
		S.C/S.T (N=38)		B.C (N=43)		F.F (N=39)		
		Mean	S.D	Mean	S.D.	Mean	S.D.	
1.	Lack of provision for honorarium to the monitors.	3.16	1.25	2.63	1.22	2.87	1.18	1.87@
2.	Lack of suitable co-operation from developmental department officials for the implementation of the decisions of the charchamandals.	3.18	1.35	2.84	1.20	3.28	0.99	1.56@
3.	Lack of provision for the production of posters and charts for the propagation of JCK activities.	3.16	1.27	3.05	1.46	3.15	1.35	0.09@
4.	Lack of suitable literacy materials for the promotion of literacy.	3.16	1.18	2.79	1.25	2.79	1.09	1.22@
5.	Lack of effective co-operation from the village leaders for implementation of the decisions of the charchamandals.	3.32	1.42	2.72	1.28	2.97	1.35	1.92@
6.	Irrelevance of the available books in JCK to the interest of adults.	3.32	1.42	2.72	1.28	2.97	1.35	1.81@
7.	Elicitation of co-operation from the village leaders.	3.26	1.58	3.21	1.61	3.23	1.56	0.01@
8.	Involvement of village politics in organising JCK activities.	3.58	1.39	3.40	1.31	3.46	1.36	0.18@
9.	The JCK activities were affected by different castes and religions.	3.71	1.47	3.65	1.38	4.18	1.24	0.75@
10.	Lack of skills among the monitors for identifying of learning problems among the adults in aquisition of literacy.	3.03	1.63	3.23	1.55	3.51	1.41	0.96@
Problem as a whole		32.24	5.63	30.28	5.08	32.21	4.61	1.93@

Note: * Significant at 0.05 level
@ Not significant at 0.05 level

Table 7: Mean and Standard Deviation Problem Scores of different occupational groups of JCK Monitors on each Item under the Area of 'Organisation' and the calculated 'f' values.

Sl.No.	Nature of the Problem	Nature of Occupation						Calculated 'f' values
		Agriculture (N=75)		Coolie (N=20)		Others (N=25)		
		Mean	S.D	Mean	S.D.	Mean	S.D.	
1.	Lack of provision for honorarium to the monitors.	2.75	1.21	3.00	1.26	3.16	1.22	1.17@
2.	Lack of suitable co-operation from developmental department officials for the implementation of the decisions of the Charcha Mandals.	3.04	1.11	3.50	1.16	2.92	1.41	1.47@
3.	Lack of provision for the production of posters and charts for the propagation of JCK activities.	3.02	1.40	2.80	1.25	3.121	.31	0.67@
4.	Lack of suitable literacy materials for the promotion of literacy.	2.83	1.16	2.75	1.08	3.28	1.22	1.58@
5.	Lack of effective co-operation from the village leaders for implementation of the decisions of the Charcha Mandals.	2.92	1.31	3.15	1.62	3.08	1.29	0.28@
6.	Irrelevance of the available books in JCK to the interest of adults.	3.07	1.28	3.45	1.43	3.52	1.06	1.55@
7.	Elicitation of co-operation from the village leaders.	3.21	1.57	3.50	1.63	3.08	1.57	0.40@
8.	Involvement of village politics in organising JCK activities.	3.31	1.40	3.55	1.16	3.92	1.23	1.98@
9.	The JCK activities were affected by different castes and religions.	3.765	1.40	4.25	1.22	3.76	1.39	1.04@
10.	Lack of skills among the monitors for identifying of learning problems among the adults in aquisition of literacy.	3.40	1.53	2.65	1.62	3.32	1.41	1.89@
	Problem as a whole	30.96	5.16	30.35	5.39	32.59	4.97	1.18@

Note ; 8 Significant at 0.05 level.
@ Not significant at 0.05 level.

Table 8: Mean and Standard Deviation Problem Scores of different income groups of JCK Monitors on each Item under the Area of 'Organisation' and the calculated 'f' values.

Sl.No.	Nature of the Problem	Income						Calculated 'f' values
		Low (N=30)		Moderate (N=51)		More (N=39)		
		Mean	S.D	Mean	S.D.	Mean	S.D.	
1.	Lack of provision for honorarium to the monitors.	3.13	1.18	2.88	1.22	2.67	1.27	1.21@
2.	Lack of suitable co-operation from developmental department officials for the implementation of the decisions of the Charcha Mandals.	2.97	1.28	3.22	1.26	3.03	1.05	0.48@
3.	Lack of provision for the production of posters and charts for the propagation of JCK activities.	3.20	1.28	3.20	1.43	2.95	1.34	0.43@
4.	Lack of suitable literacy materials for the promotion of literacy.	2.73	1.09	3.10	1.35	2.79	0.99	1.14@
5.	Lack of effective co-operation from the village leaders for implementation of the decisions of the Charcha Mandals.	2.83	1.37	3.18	1.28	2.87	1.45	0.81@
6.	Irrelevance of the available books in JCK to the interest of adults.	2.93	1.41	3.25	1.28	3.41	1.13	1.19@
7.	Eliciatation of co-operation from the village leaders.	3.27	1.29	3.65	1.53	2.67	1.68	4.44*
8.	Involvement of village politics in organising JCK activities.	3.50	1.41	3.65	1.27	3.23	1.39	1.04@
9.	The JCK activities were affected by different castes and religions.	3.87	1.28	3.86	1.40	3.79	1.44	0.03@
10.	Lack of skills among the monitors for identifying of learning problems among the adults in aquisition of literacy.	3.60	1.33	3.34	1.55	3.03	1.64	1.17@
Problem as a whole		31.17	5.68	32.27	4.96	30.87	5.00	0.84@

Note: Significant at 0.05 level.
@ Not significant at 0.05 level.

Influence of the Occupation of the JCK Monitors on their problems in the Area of Organisation.

In Table–7 presents the mean and S.D. scores of different occupational groups of JCK monitors under the area of organisation as a whole and each item and calculated 'F, values.

The results presented in the Table–7 discloses that the monitors belonging to the occupations-Agriculture, Coolie and others does not differ significantly with each other with regard to the problems in the area of organisation. However, the trend of obtaining the problem mean score reveals that the monitors from agricultural background who have related problems with regard to the organisation of JCKs were found to be easier than the monitors from collie and other work groups. The calculated F, value is also not significant.

The itemwise analysis of the monitor problems in the area of organisation, also showed in the table reveals that the monitors of these three groups do not differ significantly with each other in the area. In otherwords monitors of all the three groups viewed the problems under organisation of JCKs similarly. Hence, the hypothesis " There is no significant difference in each problem and problems as a whole faced by JCK monitors under the area of organisation of JCK activities due to variations in their occupation is accepted.

Influence of JCK Monitors Income on their Problems in the Area of Organisation

In order to study the influence of income on the problems of the monitor in the area of organisation, the monitors were classified into three groups–low, Moderate and More income groups. The further analysis done with regard to the item in the area was presented in the Table-8.

The result presented in Table-8 reveals that the monitors belonging to less and more experienced groups differ significantly on two items namely, lack of provision for the production of posters and charts for the propagation of JCK activities and they do not differ on the rest of the items. The trend of the obtained mean scores of the monitors on significant items reveals that the monitors with less experience felt that implementation of Charcha Mandal decisions without the co-operation of the officials is very difficult. On the other hand, monitors with less experience are of the opinion that caste and religion of the participants obstruct the implementation of the various activities of the JCK. It is true that the practice of the caste is more prevalent in rural areas and hence the monitors are facing the same. Further, the guidelines of the JCKs clearly envisage the co-operation from developmental departments in various activities of the JCKs. However, it appears in practice the help is not forthcoming. Hence the programme implementors should take effective measures to eradicate the influence of the caste and elicitation of more co-operation form the officials of developmental departments.

The Itemwise analysis of the problems in the area of organisation of the JCKs presented in the Table–8 discloses that the monitors of these three groups differ significantly on one item namely elicitation of co-operation from village leaders. The obtained item mean score reveals that monitors with moderate income group felt the item as more prominent problem followed by less and more income groups of monitors. However, the monitors do not differ from each other with regard to the rest of the items. In view of the above the hypothesis, " There is no significant difference between each problem and problem as a whole faced by JCK Monitor under the area of organisation of JCK activities due to variation in their income" is rejected only in the case of the item elicitation of co-operation from village leaders and accepted in case of other items.

Influence of the Experience of JCK Monitors on their problems in the Area of Organisation

In Table–9 the mean and S.Ds. of the problem scores of More experienced and Less experienced JCK monitors and the calculated 't' values are presented.

The result presented in the Table–9 discloses that the monitors with less and more experience in the field of Adult Education do not differ each other in the problem area organisation of the JCK. The trend of the obtained problem score also reveals that the difference between mean scores is not insignificant. Hence the formulated hypothesis, " There is no significant difference in each problem and problem as a whole faced by JCK monitor under the area of

Table– 9: Mean and Standard Deviation Problem Score of both experience groups of JCK Monitors on each Item under the Area of 'Organisation' and the calculated t' values.

Sl.No.	Nature of the Problem	Experience				Calculated 't' values
		Less (N=64)		More (N=56)		
		Mean	S.D	Mean	S.D.	
1.	Lack of provision for honorarium to the monitors.	2.80	1.27	2.94	1.20	0.60@
2.	Lack of suitable co-operation from relevant officials for the implementation of the decisions of the Charcha Mandals.	2.89	1.16	3.27	1.22	1.72@
3.	Lack of provision for the production of posters and Charts for the propagation of JCK activities.	2.79	1.26	3.41	1.39	2.56@
4.	Lack of suitable literacy materials for the promotion of literacy.	2.93	1.25	2.89	1.13	0.17@
5.	Lack of suitable literacy materials for the promotion of literacy.	2.86	1.39	3.11	1.34	1.01@
6.	Irrelevance of the available books in JCK to the interest of adults.	3.21	1.31	3.23	1.26	0.09@
7.	Elicitation of co-operation from the village leaders.	3.05	1.60	3.39	1.56	1.17*
8.	Involvement of village politics in organising JCK activities.	3.36	1.39	3.58	1.31	0.89@
9.	The JCK activities were affected by different castes and religions.	3.82	1.39	3.86	1.38	0.15@
10.	Lack of skills among the monitors for identifying of learning problems among the adults in aquisition of literacy	3.57	1.35	2.98	1.65	2.14*
Problem as a whole		3.16	5.01	31.84	5.35	0.72@

Note: * Significant at 0.05 level.
@ Not significant at 0.05 level.

organisation of JCK activities due to variations in their Experience" is accepted.

Influence of the Educational status of the monitors on their problems in the Area of Organisation.

The result presented in the Table–10 discloses that the monitors with different levels of education have obtained more or less similar mean problem score in the problem area of organisation of JCK. However, the obtained mean problem score of the area reveals that monitors with moderate level of education perceived it as more problematic than the other groups. Surprisingly, the monitors with low level of education rated the area as low problematic area. The results presented in the table also disclose that out of ten items, the monitors with three levels of education differ significantly on three of the items namely lack of provision for the production of posters and charts for the propagation of JCK activities, Irrelevancy of available books in JCKs to the interests of adults and involvement of village politics in organising JCK activities. The trend of the obtained mean problems score reveal that the monitors with low level of education have as rated in all the three items were less problamatic. On the other hand, the monitors with more level of education as rated in item three and six as more problematic and the monitors with moderate level of education as rated in item eight as prominent problem. In view of the above, the programme administrators should take steps to provide relevant literature to JCKs and provision may be made for popularisation of JCK activities in the community and people may persuaded not to club the politics with JCK activities. In view of the above the hypothesis "There is no significant difference in each problem and problem as a whole faced by JCK monitor under the area of organisation of JCK activities due to variations in their educational status" is accepted, except in the case of the three items-lack of provision for the production of posters and charts for the propagation of JCK activities, irrelevancy of available books in JCK to the interest of adults and involvement of village politics in organising JCK activities.

Table–10 Mean and Standard Deviation Problem Scores of different educational groups of JCK Monitors on each Item under the Area of 'Organisation' and the calculated 'f' values.

Sl.No.	Nature of the Problem	Education						Calculated 'f' values
		Low (N=20)		Moderate (N=77)		More (N=23)		
		Mean	S.D	Mean	S.D.	Mean	S.D.	
1.	Lack of provision for honorarium to the monitors.	3.15	1.31	2.90	1.26	2.57	0.97	1.22@
2.	Lack of suitable co-operation from relevant officials for the implementation of the decisions of the Charcha Mandals.	2.80	1.08	3.13	1.29	3.22	0.93	0.74@
3.	Lack of provision for the production of posters and charts for the propagation of JCK activities.	2.70	1.23	3.08	1.42	3.61	1.13	2.49*
4.	Lack of suitable literacy materials for the promotion of literacy.	3.05	1.32	2.95	1.19	2.65	1.00	0.71@
5.	Lack of effective co-operation from the village leaders for implementation of the decisions of the Charcha Mandals.	2.50	1.24	3.13	1.41	2.96	1.23	1.69@
6.	Irrelevance of the available books in JCK to the interest of adults.	2.60	1.07	3.31	1.34	3.48	1.06	3.09*
7.	Elicitation of co-operation from the village leaders.	2.85	1.74	3.38	1.55	3.09	1.47	0.99@
8.	Involvement of village politics in organising JCK activities.	3.00	1.38	3.65	1.32	3.30	1.33	2.08@
9.	The JCK activities were affected by different castes and religions.	3.70	1.49	3.84	1.40	3.96	1.23	0.18*
10.	Lack of skills among the monitors for identifying of							

learning problems among the adults in aquisition of literacy.	3.40	1.28	3.22	1.62	3.26	1.48	0.14@
Problem as a whole	29.90	5.20	31.90	5.44	31.70	3.99	1.17@

Note: * Significant at 0.05 level.
@ Not significant at 0.05 level.

Influence of the Marital Status of JCK Monitors on their problems in the Organisation of JCK activities

The results presented in the Table 11 with regard to the influence of marital status of JCK monitors on their problems in the area of organisation of the JCKs discloses that married and unmarried monitors experienced the problems similarly and do not differ significantly from each other. The further analysis was also done to study the influence of the marital status and different items in the area of organisation are presented in the Table–11.

The result presented in the Table–11 also discloses that married and unmarried monitors do not differ from each other on al the items. It appears that there is no specific problem associated with the marital status. Hence, the hypothesis " There is no significant difference in each problem and problem as a whole faced by JCK monitor under the area of organisation of JCK activities due to variations in their marital status" is accepted.

Influence of Personal Characteristics of the Monitors on their Problems in the Area of Administration

In order to identify the influence of the monitors characteristics on their problems in the area of Administration, eight problems were included in the area. Out of these eight, three items were found to be prominent problems and two of the items were found to be moderate problems. The prominent problems of the area namely–the traditional beliefs and customs are becoming obstacle in organising JCK activities relating to women empowerment, Accommodating representatives of various groups in village level literacy committee and working monitors age and experience do not suit for discussion of village problems in Charcha Mandals. Items such as–lack of information on developmental programmes and Charcha Mandal activities affected due to village politics, were found to be moderate problems. Hence efforts must be made to solve the problems by the programme administrators for enhancing the quality of the programme.

In order to bring out the nature of influence of the characteristics on the Administrative problems, detailed analysis, areawise and itemwise was done and presented in the following pages.

Table 11: Mean and Standard Deviation Problem Scores of both marital status groups of JCK Monitors on each Item under the Area of 'Organisation' and the calculated t' values.

Sl.No.	Nature of the Problem	Marital Status				Calculated 't' values
		Married (N=63)		Un-married (N=57)		
		Mean	S.D	Mean	S.D.	
1.	Lack of provision for honorarium to the monitors.	2.81	1.28	2.95	1.18	0.61@
2.	Lack of suitable co-operation from relevant officials for the implementation of the decisions of the Charcha Mandals.	3.00	1.07	3.19	1.33	0.87@
3.	Lack of provision for the production of posters and charts for the propagation of JCK activities.	3.06	1.40	3.18	1.33	0.45@
4.	Lack of suitable literacy materials for the promotion of literacy.	2.33	1.11	3.00	1.27	0.81@
5.	Lack of effective co-operation from the village leaders for implementation of the decisions of the Charcha Mandals.	2.94	3.05	1.28	1.46	0.46@
6.	Irrelevance of the available books in JCK to the interest of adults.	3.32	1.21	3.12	1.35	0.83@
7.	Elicitation of co-operation from the village leaders.	3.13	1.62	3.35	1.54	0.78@
8.	Involvement of village politics in organising JCK activities.	3.52	1.28	3.42	1.43	0.41@
9.	The JCK activities were affected by different castes and religions.	3.75	1.40	3.95	1.36	0.81@

10.	Lack of skills among the monitors for identifying of learning problems among the adults in aquisition of literacy.	3.32	1.48	3.19	1.62	0.44@
Problem as a whole		31.33	4.98	31.74	5.43	0.421@

Note : * Significant at 0.05 level.
@ Not significant at 0.05 level.

Influence of Sex of the JCK Monitors on their problems in the Area of Administration

In order to identify the influence of sex on different administration problems of JCK, a thorough item wise analysis were made and presented in Table –12.

The list of the problems, total mean of the item, Mean, S.Ds. and 't', values obtained by men and women monitors are presented in Table–12.

From the above table it is clear that men and women were found to be significantly different on the item—taking special care for the backward learners. The trend of the obtained mean problem score reveals that women were found to be feeling difficult in taking special care for backward learners. On rest of the items, the men and women monitors do not significantly differ from each other on Administration problems. Hence, the hypothesis " There is no significant difference in each problem and problem as a whole faced by JCK monitor under the area Administration of JCk activities due to variations in their sex" is accepted, accepted, except in case of the item taking special care for backward learners.

Influence of the Caste of JCk Monitors on their Problems in the Area of Administration

In order to study the influence of the caste on Administration problems, the monitors were classified in three groups namely SC/ ST, B.C. and F.C groups and itemwise analysis was also done and presented in the Table—13.

The result presented in the Table—13 shows that the monitors of the three caste groups do not differ significantly from each other. However, the trend of the obtained mean problems scores reveals that the monitors with B.C. background have rated Administration problems as less prominent problems. The monitor belonging to S.C./ S.T and F. C. groups have rated in a similar way. Keeping the above in view, the itemwise analysis were also made. The list of the items, item mean score, S.D. and 'F' - values obtained by the monitors belonging to different caste groups were also presented in the Table–13.

Table 12: Mean and Standard Deviation Problem Scores of both sex groups of JCk Monitors on each Item under the Area of 'Administration' and the calculated 't', values.

Sl.No.	Nature of the Problem	Sex				Calculated 'f' values
		Men (N=60)		Women (N=60)		
		Mean	S.D	Mean	S.D.	
1.	Lack of suitable sports and games materials at the JCK	2.95	1.50	2.90	1.51	0.18@
2.	Lack of information on developmental programmes.	3.15	1.29	3.17	1.29	0.07@
3.	Inability in providing different occupational skills to neo-literates.	3.58	1.50	4.03	1.45	1.67@
4.	The traditional beliefs and customs are becoming obstacles in organising JCK activities relating to women empowerment.	2.80	1.33	2.97	1.21	0.71@
5.	Charchamandal activities were affected due to village politics.	3.55	1.56	3.32	1.49	0.83@
6.	Taking special care of the backward learners.	3.72	1.53	4.25	1.27	2.07*
7.	Accommodating representatives of various groups in village level literacy committee	2.93	1.46	2.55	1.49	1.42@
8.	The Working monitors' age and experience does not suit for discussion of village problems in Charcha Mandals.	3.60	1.38	3.87	1.33	1.07@
Problem as a whole		26.28	5.73	27.05	4.89	0.78@

Note : * Significant at 0.05 level.
@ Not significant at 0.05 level.

Table–13: Mean and Standard Deviation Problem Scores of different caste groups of JCK Monitors on each item under the Area of 'Administration' and the calculated 'f' values.

Sl.No.	Nature of the Problem	Caste						Calculated 'f' values
		S.C/S.T (N=38)		B.C. (N=43)		F.C. (N=39)		
		Mean	S.D	Mean	S.D.	Mean	S.D.	
1.	Lack of suitable sports and games materials at the JCK	2.89	1.45	2.70	1.45	3.21	1.59	1.16@
2.	Lack of information on developmental programmes.	3.34	1.32	2.86	1.25	3.31	1.24	1.80@
3.	Inability in providing different occupational skills to neo-literates.	3.87	1.34	3.63	1.56	3.95	1.54	0.51@
4.	The traditional beliefs and customs are becoming obstacles in organising activites relating to the women empowerment.	2.84	1.35	2.93	1.21	2.87	1.26	0.04@
5.	Charcha Mandal activities were affected due to village politics.	3.58	1.53	3.19	1.56	3.56	1.46	0.86@
6.	Taking special cafe the backward learners.	3.87	1.54	3.95	1.40	4.13	1.34	0.32@
7.	Accommodating representatives of various groups in village level literacy committee.	2.68	1.45	3.02	1.59	2.49	1.34	1.36
8.	The working monitors age and experience does not suit for discussion of village problems in Charcha Mandals.	3.95	1.15	3.33	1.52	3.97	1.27	3.07*
Problem as a whole		27.03	5.41	25.60	5.39	27.49	5.02	1.39@

Note : * Significant at 0.05 level.
@ Not significant at 0.05 level.

The result presented in the table discloses that the monitors of these groups differ significantly from each other on the items namely-working monitors age and experience does not suit for discussion of village problems in Charcha Mandals. The obtained mean problem score reveals that the S.C/.S.T and F.C. groups of monitors felt the item as prominent problem, whereas the monitors with backward caste background have rated the item as less prominent problem. The monitors of these three groups do not significantly differ on the rest of the items. Hence, the hypothesis "There is no significant difference in each problem as a whole faced by JCK monitors under the area Administration of JCK activities due to variation in their caste" is accepted except in case of the problems- working monitors age and experience does not suit for discussion of village problems in Charcha Mandals.

Influence of the Occupation of the JCK Monitors on their problems in the Area of Administration

The results presented in Table–14 reveals that, the monitors representing different occupational groups does not differ significantly from each other. The trend of obtained mean problems scores indicated that the monitors with backward caste background rated it as a less prominent problem and the monitors with forward caste background rated it as a prominent problem. Keeping the above results in view, a probe was made to bring out the nature of the influence of the characteristics of the monitors on Administration problems by way of itemwise analysis.

The result presented in the Table–14 also discloses that the monitors with different occupational backgrounds differ significantly on the item–lack of suitable sports and games material for JCK. The trend of the obtained problem mean score reveals that the monitors with Agricultural background rated it as a less prominent problem. On the otherhand, monitors with un-employed background rated it as a prominent problem. These three groups of monitors do not differ significantly from each other on the rest of the items. Hence, the hypothesis "There is no significant difference in each problem and problem as a whole faced by JCK monitor under the area. Administration of JCK activities due to variations in their occupation" is accepted except in case of item–lack of suitable sports and games material in the JCK.

Table– 14 : Mean and Standard Deviation Problem Scores of different occupational groups of JCK Monitors on each item under the Area of 'Administration' and the calculated 't' values.

Sl.No.	Nature of the Problem	Occupation						Calculated 't' values
		Agriculture (N=75)		Cooling (N=20)		Others (N=25)		
		Mean	S.D	Mean	S.D.	Mean	S.D.	
1.	Lack of suitable sports and games materials at the JCK	2.63	1.48	3.25	1.41	3.56	1.42	4.35*
2.	Lack of information on developmental programmes.	3.03	1.30	3.20	1.33	3.52	1.17	1.37@
3.	Inability in providing different occupational skills to neo-literates.	3.77	1.51	3.70	1.55	4.00	1.36	0.27@
4.	The traditional beliefs and customs are becoming- obstacles in organising JCK activities relating to the women empowerment.	2.97	1.25	2.75	1.13	2.72	1.40	0.49@
5.	Charcha Mandal activities were affected due to village politics.	3.39	1.58	3.15	1.49	3.80	1.33	1.08@
6.	Taking special care of the backward learners.	3.88	1.51	4.25	1.04	4.08	1.44	0.59@
7.	Accommodating representatives of various groups in village level literacy committee.	2.69	1.50	3.25	1.41	2.48	1.42	1.60@
8.	The working monitors age and experience does not suit for discussion of village problem in Charcha Mandals.	3.67	1.37	3.75	1.41	3.92	1.29	0.31@
Problem as a whole		26.03	5.70	27.30	4.18	28.08	4.69	1.55@

Note : * Significant at 0.05 level.
@ Not significant at 0.05 level.

The influence of JCK Monitors Income on their problems in the Area of Administration

Based on the income of the monitors, monitors were classified into three groups (low, Middle and More), for identifying the influence of income on their Administration problems in organising JCKs and the results are presented in Table–15.

The result presented in the Table–15 shows that, the monitors belonging to less, moderate and more income groups differ significantly from each other on Administration problems in the organisation of the jCKs. The obtained mean problem scores of monitors reveal that the moderate income group monitors rated the area as more problematic followed by more and less income groups. Further analysis were also done in the form of item analysis.

The item wise analysis reveals that the monitors belonging to less, moderate and more income groups differ significantly on the items –involvement of village politics in Charcha Mandal activities and taking special care of backward learners. The trend of obtained problem score of the above two items discloses that the monitors with moderate income groups have rated the above items as prominent problems, whereas this group of monitors does not differ significantly from each other and rest of the items. In view of the above the hypothesis "There is no significant difference in each problem and problem as a whole faced by JCK monitor under area Administration of JCK activities due to variations in their income" is accepted except in case of the above two items.

The Influence of the Experience of JCK Monitors on their problems in the Area of Administration

Based on the years of experience the monitors were classified into less experienced and more experienced. Then an attempt was made to identify the influence of experience on the administrative problems of the monitors in the organisation of JCKs.

Table–15: Mean and Standard Deviation Problem Scores of different income groups of JCK Monitors on each item under the Area of 'Administration' and the calculated 'f' values.

Sl.No.	Nature of the Problem	Income						Calculated 'f' values
		Low (N=30)		Middle (N=51)		More (N=39)		
		Mean	S.D	Mean	S.D.	Mean	S.D.	
1.	Lack of suitable sports and games materials at the JCK	2.90	1.58	3.00	1.46	2.85	1.51	0.11@
2.	Lack of information on developmental programmes.	3.10	1.27	3.33	1.29	2.97	1.27	0.88@
3.	Inability in providing different occupational skills to neo-literates.	3.63	1.49	4.08	1.25	3.59	1.71	1.46@
4.	The traditional beliefs and customs are becoming-obstacles in organising JCK activities relating to the women empowerment.	2.67	1.14	2.98	1.35	2.92	1.25	0.59@
5.	Charchamandal activities were affected due to village politics.	3.53	1.31	3.73	1.53	2.97	1.58	2.80*
6.	Taking special care of the backward learners.	3.53	1.36	4.22	1.36	4.03	1.49	2.80*
7.	Accommodating representatives of various groups in village level literacy committee.	2.80	1.22	2.71	1.64	2.74	1.46	0.03@
8.	The working monitors' age and experience does not suit for discussion of village problems in Charcha Mandals.	3.37	1.40	3.92	1.20	3.77	1.48	1.58@
Problem as a whole		25.47	5.30	27.96	4.92	25.90	5.54	2.71*

Note: * Significant at 0.05 level.
@ Not significant at 0.05 level.

Table–16 discloses that the mean problem score difference is not significant as the calculated 't' values is lesser than the table value. In view of the above results, further analysis were made to bring out the nature of the relationship between the characteristics of the problem.

The results presented in the Table–16 reveals that the monitors with less and more experience does not differ from each other significantly as the mean difference is negligible in case of all the items. From the above it appears that the monitors of less and more experienced groups experience the Administrative problems similarly. Hence the hypothesis " There is no significant difference in each problem and problem as a whole faced by JCK monitor under the area Administration of JCK activities due to variation in their experience" is accepted.

The Influence of Educational Status of JCk Monitors on their Administrative Problems

To bring out the influence of education on Administrative problems of the monitors, the monitors were classified into three groups–low, moderate and more education level groups and Anova technic was applied to find out the differences if any among these groups.

The results presented in the Table–17 discloses that the difference between these three groups were found to be not significant and the calculated F-value is less than the table value. Further analysis was also made in the form of item analysis and the results were presented in the same table.

The result presented in the table discloses that the monitors belonging to three different levels of education do not differ significantly with each other as the mean differences were very low. In otherwords, monitors of all these groups felt similarly about the administrative problems in the organisation of JCKs and no specific problem is associated with the level of education. In view of the above the stated hypothesis " There is no significant difference in each problem and problem as a whole faced by JCK monitor under the area Administration of JCK activities due to variation in their Educational status is accepted.

Table–16: Mean and Standard Deviation Problem Scores of both Experience groups of JCK Monitors on each item under the Area of 'Administration' and the calculated 't' values.

Sl.No.	Nature of the Problem	Experience: Less (N=56) Mean	Less (N=56) S.D	Experience: More (N=64) Mean	More (N=64) S.D.	Calculated 't' values
1.	Lack of suitable sports and games materials at the JCK	2.77	1.45	3.06	1.54	1.07@
2.	Lack of information on developmental programmes.	3.14	1.19	3.17	1.38	0.12@
3.	Inability in providing different occupational skills to neo-literates.	3.91	1.46	3.72	1.52	0.70@
4.	The traditional beliefs and customs are becoming obstacles in organising JCK activities relating to the women empowerment.	2.96	1.27	2.81	1.27	0.65@
5.	Charchamandal activities were affected due to village politics.	3.46	1.46	3.41	1.59	0.20@
6.	Taking special care of the backward learners.	3.84	1.47	4.11	1.38	1.03@
7.	Accommodating representatives of various groups in village level literacy committee.	2.75	1.47	2.73	1.50	0.05@
8.	The working monitors' age and experience does not suit for discussion of village problems in Charcha Mandals.	3.70	1.29	3.77	1.42	0.27@
Problem as a whole		26.57	4.98	26.75	5.64	0.18@

Note: * Significant at 0.05 level.
@ Not significant at 0.05 level.

Table–17: Mean and Standard Deviation Problem Scores of different education groups of JCK Monitors on each item under the Area of 'Administration' and the calculated 'f' values.

Sl.No.	Nature of the Problem	Education						Calculated 'f' values
		Low (N=20)		Middle (N=77)		More (N=23)		
		Mean	S.D	Mean	S.D.	Mean	S.D.	
1.	Lack of suitable sports and games materials at the JCK	2.50	1.20	2.99	1.53	3.09	1.59	0.98@
2.	Lack of information on developmental programmes.	3.15	1.19	3.04	1.33	3.57	1.14	1.47@
3.	Inability in providing different occupational skills to neo-literates.	3.95	1.47	3.92	1.38	3.30	1.73	1.63@
4.	The traditional beliefs and customs are becoming - obstacles in organising JCK activities relating to the women empowerment.	3.00	1.22	2.81	1.24	3.04	1.40	0.40@
5.	Charcha Mandal activities were affected due to village politics.	3.40	1.39	3.57	1.51	3.00	1.64	1.23@
6.	Taking special care of the backward learners.	3.75	1.48	3.96	1.48	4.26	1.15	0.69@
7.	Accommodating representatives of various groups in village level literacy committee.	3.00	1.45	2.69	1.48	2.70	1.52	0.35@
8.	The working monitors' age and experience does not suit for discussion of village problems in Charcha Mandals.	3.70	1.42	3.69	1.33	3.91	1.41	0.24@
Problem as a whole		26.45	4.90	26.66	5.46	26.87	5.29	0.03@

Note : * Significant at 0.05 level.
@ Not significant at 0.05 level.

The Influence of the Marital Status on the Administrative problems of the JCK Monitors

In order to study the influence of marital status on the Administrative problems of the JCK, the monitors were classified accordingly and 't'- test was applied.

The results presented in the Table–18 reveals that the mean differences between the married and un-married monitors is nill and not significant. Further analysis were also made to identify the differences if any between these groups on each Administrative problem items.

The results presented in the Table–18 discloses that married and un-married monitors do not differ significantly on any of the problem items listed under Administrative problems. Hence the hypothesis "There is no significant difference in each problem and problem as a whole faced by JCK monitor under the area of Administration of JCK activities due to variation in their Marital status" is accepted.

The Influence of the Selected Characteristics of the Monitors on their Problems in the Area of Environment of the JCK

The intention of the unit is to study the influence of personal characteristics of the monitors on the problems in the area of creation of proper environment for successful organisation of JCK activities. The collected data was analysed, interpreted and presented in tables.

Out of the 38 listed problems 6 of the problems were found to be related to the creation of environment for the programme. As per the criterion of Mean ± ½ S.D. Out of the six problems of the environment three items were found to be moderate problems and an equal number of the items were found to be less prominant category. Inspite of importance of the area in successful implementation of the programme, not even a single problem was identified as prominent problem. Hence, it appears that the working monitors were not facing any problems with regard to the environment. It may be probably due to the fact that the Total Literacy Campaign Authorities of the district have taken the task of creation of the environment for successful implementation of the programme.

Table–18 : Mean and Standard Deviation Problem Scores of both Marital status groups of JCK Monitors on each item under the Area of 'Administration' and the calculated 't' values.

Sl.No.	Nature of the Problem	Marital Status				Calculated 't' values
		Married (N=63)		Unmarried (N=57)		
		Mean	S.D	Mean	S.D.	
1.	Lack of suitable sports and games materials at the JCK	3.03	1.56	2.81	1.43	0.82@
2.	Lack of information on developmental programmes.	3.25	1.22	3.05	1.36	0.85@
3.	Inability in providing different occupational skills to neo-literates.	3.75	1.59	3.88	1.36	0.48@
4.	The traditional beliefs and customs are becoming obstacles in organising JCK activities relating to the women empowerment.	2.71	1.27	3.07	1.25	1.54@
5.	Charchamandal activities were affected due to village politics.	3.40	1.50	3.47	1.57	0.27@
6.	Taking special care of the backward learners.	3.97	1.50	4.00	1.34	0.12@
7.	Accommodating representatives of various groups in village level literacy committee.	2.79	1.52	2.68	1.44	0.40@
8.	The working monitors age and experience does not suit for discussion of village problems in Charcha Mandals.	3.76	1.37	3.70	1.36	0.24@
Problem as a whole		26.67	5.29	26.67	54.0	0.00@

Note: * Significant at 0.05 level.
@ Not significant at 0.05 level.

In addition to above, the collected data was analysed to study the influence of personal characteristics of the monitors on the problem of creation of environment and the results were presented in the form of tables.

The Influence of the Sex of the JCK Monitors on their Environmental Problems in the organisation of JCK activities

The results presented in the Table–19 discloses that the monitors belonging to men and women group do not differ significantly in the area of creation of environment for JCK activities. However, the trend of the obtained problem mean score of the area of the two groups shows that men were found to be facing more problems than women in creation of the environment.

Further analysis was also done to analyse the relationship between sex and problems relating to the creation of environment and the results along with the list of the items, total means score of the item, mean, S.D., 't', values obtained by the men and women monitors were presented in Table–19.

From the Table–19 it appears that men and women monitors do not differ significantly with each other on all the items except on the item choosing a convenient place for organisation of JCK. The trend of the mean score of the item obtained by men and women monitors discloses that men monitors were found to be facing more problems than women monitors with regard to the creation of suitable place.

In view of the above hypothesis "There is no significant difference in each problem and problem as a whole faced by JCK monitor under the area of environment of JCK activities due to variations in their sex" is accepted except in case of the item choosing a convenient place for organisation of JCK.

The Influence of Caste of the JCK Monitors on their problems in the Area Creation of Environment

The result relating to the influence of caste of the monitor on the problem of creation of environment is presented in Table–20.

Table–19 : Mean and Standard Deviation Problem Scores of both, sex groups of JCK Monitors on each item under the Area of 'Environment' and the calculated 't', values.

Sl.No.	Nature of the Problem	Sex: Men (N=60) Mean	Men (N=60) S.D	Women (N=60) Mean	Women (N=60) S.D.	Calculated 't' values
1.	Lack of audio-visual aids to disseminate the information to the learners in JCK	3.02	1.53	2.60	1.40	1.55@
2.	Ability to maintain hormonious relationship with the villagers.	3.13	1.45	2.92	1.37	0.84@
3.	Lack of equal participation on the part of men and women in the activities of JCK	2.53	1.55	3.07	1.44	1.95@
4.	The standard of language in the available reading materials in JCK is higher than the learniner's standard.	3.48	1.37	3.20	1.41	1.11@
5.	Ability to motivate the Neo-literates for continuing education.	3.42	1.43	3.00	1.53	1.54@
6.	Choosing a suitable place for effective learning.	3.40	1.33	2.85	1.39	2.21*
	Problem as a whole	18.98	4.81	17.63	4.36	1.61@

Note : * Significant at 0.5 level.
@ Not significant at 0.05 level.

The table shows that monitors with different caste backgrounds differ significantly from each other. The obtained trend of the mean problem score of the area by the three caste groups of the monitors discloses that the monitors belonging to forward caste group felt it as prominent problem followed by S.C/S.T and B.C. groups.

In the itemwise analysis, it is also revealed that the three caste groups differ significantly from each other on the item-lack of equal participation of men and women in the activities of the JCK. The trend of the obtained mean problem score of the item shows that forward caste groups were not able to generate equal participation of men and women in the activities of JCK . It is true that most of F.C. groups belonging to middle class families under strictly practising the traditional beliefs and customs and as a result the JCKs organised by this group for the middle class families may be facing this problem. Hence, the programme administrators should take effective steps to overcome the above problem.

In view of the results obtained the stated Hypothesis "There is no significant difference in each problem and problem as a whole face by JCK monitor under the area of environment of JCK activities due to variations in their sex" is accepted except in case of the item choosing a convenient place for organisation of JCK.

The Influence of the Occupational Status of JCK Monitors on their Problems in the Area of Environment

The results relating to the influence of occupation of the monitor on their problems in creation of environment is presented in Table–21. The findings indicates that the monitors with different backgrounds does not differ significantly from each other as the difference between the calculated problem mean score of these three groups is very less. In otherwords, all the three groups of monitors experienced the same sort of the problems in creating environment for implementation of JCK. In view of the above, further analysis in the form of item analysis was made.

The findings presented in the table discloses that these three groups of monitors do not differ significantly on 5 of the 6 items and differ significantly only on one item *i.e.*, lack of audio-visual aids in

Table–20: Mean and Standard Deviation Problem Scores of different caste groups of JCK Monitors on each Item under the Area of 'Environment' and the calculated 'f' values.

Sl.No.	Nature of the Problem	Caste						Calculated 'f' values
		S.C/S/T (N=38)		B.C. (N=43)		F.C. (N=39)		
		Mean	S.D	Mean	S.D.	Mean	S.D.	
1.	Lack of audio-visual aids to dissiminate the information to the learners in JCK	2.92	1.56	2.53	1.30	3.00	1.55	1.15@
2.	Ability to maintain hormonious relationship with the villagers.	2.95	1.49	2.93	1.34	3.21	1.42	0.46@
3.	Lack of equal participation on the part of men and women in the activities of JCK	2.55	1.57	2.56	1.48	3.31	1.38	3.32*
4.	The standard of language in the available reading materials in JCK is higher than the learners' standard.	3.45	1.53	3.14	1.30	3.46	1.24	0.69@
5.	Ability to motivate the Neo-literates for continuing education.	3.47	1.63	2.98	1.37	3.21	1.44	1.10@
6.	Choosing a suitable place for effective learning.	3.34	1.20	2.88	1.40	3.18	1.50	1.13@
Problem as a whole		18.68	4.09	17.02	4.93	19.36	4.48	2.83*

Note: * Significant at 0.05 level.
@ Not significant at 0.05 level.

Table–21: Mean and Standard Deviation Problem Score of different occupational groups of JCK Monitors on each Item under the Area of 'Environment' and the calculated 'f' values.

Sl.No.	Nature of the Problem	Occupation						Calculated 'f' values
		Agriculture (N=75)		Coolie (N=20)		Others (N=25)		
		Mean	S.D	Mean	S.D.	Mean	S.D.	
1.	Lack of audio-visual aids to dissiminate the information to the learners in JCK	2.67	1.45	3.45	1.53	2.72	1.40	2.28*
2.	Ability to maintain hormonious relationship with the villagers.	2.95	1.49	2.93	1.34	3.21	1.42	0.30@
3.	Lack of equal participation on the part of men and women in the activities of JCK	2.55	1.57	2.56	1.48	3.31	1.38	0.76@
4.	The standard of language in the available reading materials in JCK is higher than the learners' standard.	3.45	1.53	3.14	1.30	3.46	1.24	0.17@
5.	Ability to motivate the Neo-literates for continuing education	3.47	1.63	2.98	1.37	3.21	1.44	5.86*
6.	Choosing a suitable place for effective learning.	3.34	1.20	2.88	1.40	3.18	1.50	0.73@
Problem as a whole		17.76	4.83	20.05	4.31	18.56	3.90	1.98*

Note : * Significant at 0.05 level.
@ Not significant at 0.05 level.

JCKs. The trend of the obtained problem mean score reveals that only the monitors belonging to labour group felt it as a predominant problem than the other two groups. In view of the above results the hypothesis "There is no significant difference in each problem and problem as a whole faced by JCK monitor under the area of Environment of JCK activities due to variations in their occupation" is accepted except in case of item lack of audio-visual aids in JCKs.

The Influence of JCK Monitors Income on their Problems in the Area of Environment

The results indicating the influence of income on the environmental problems of JCK monitors are presented in Table–22.

The monitors belonging to different income groups do not differ significantly from each other in Table–22. In otherwords, the influence of the income of the monitors is not related to the problems that they have experienced in creation of environmental aspects of the programme.

The further analysis made in Table–22 also reveals that the monitors with low, middle and more income groups do not differ significantly on all the six items listed under environment. In view of the above results the hypothesis " There is no significant difference in each problem and problem as a whole faced by JCK monitor under the area Environment of JCk activities due to variations in their Income" is accepted.

The Influence of the Experience of the JCK Monitors on their Environmental Problems

The findings relating to the influence of the experience of the monitors on the problems relating to the environment are presented in the Table–23. In Table–23 the monitors with less and more experience do not differ significantly with each other as the difference between obtained mean problem score of these three groups were very minimal. However, the trend indicates that more experienced people in adult education are experiencing more problems than the less experienced group. So in order to study this relationship in depth further analysis was also made.

Table–22: Mean and Standard Deviation Problem scores of the different Income groups of JCK Monitors on each Item under the Area of 'Environment' and the calculated 'f' values.

Sl.No.	Nature of the Problem	Education						Calculated 'f' values
		Low (N=30)		Middle (N=51)		More (N=39)		
		Mean	S.D	Mean	S.D.	Mean	S.D.	
1.	Lack of audio-visual aids to dissiminate the information to the learners in JCK	3.10	1.54	2.76	1.52	2.64	1.37	0.83@
2.	Ability to maintain hormonious relationship with the villagers.	3.13	1.41	3.04	1.48	2.92	1.33	0.18@
3.	Lack of equal participation on the part of men and wo nen in the activities of JCK	2.53	1.38	2.96	1.53	2.97	1.57	0.73@
4.	The standard of language in the available reading materials in JCK is higher than the learners standard.	3.33	1.16	3.59	1.52	3.03	1.33	1.79@
5.	Ability to motivate the Neo-literates for continuing education.	3.30	1.37	3.22	1.60	3.13	1.44	0.11@
6.	Choosing a suitable place for effective learning.	3.20	1.28	3.10	1.46	3.10	1.37	0.05@
	Problem as a whole	18.47	4.08	18.67	4.94	17.72	4.59	0.47@

Note: * Significant at 0.05 level.
@ Not significant at 0.05 level.

The itemwise results presented in the table discloses that the more and less experienced monitors do not differ with each other on the item- lack of audio-visual aids in JCK. The trend of the obtained mean problem score shows that less experienced group of monitors felt that the problem–lack of audio-visual aids is more prominant than the other group. It is true that the less experienced monitors may not be in a position to handle the literacy and literacy promotion activities effectively without audio-visual aids. Keeping in view of the above results the stated hypothesis " There is no significant difference in each problem and problem as a whole faced by JCK monitor under the area Environment of JCK activities due to variations in their Experience" is accepted except in case of the item lack of audio-visual aids in JCK.

The Influence of the Educational Status of JCK Monitors on their Environmental Problems

The influence of the level of education on these environmental problems of the monitors in the organisation of JCK activities are presented in Table–24.

The obtained F-value in Table–24 reveals that there is no significant difference in the problems faced by the monitors with different educational background.

However, the trend shows that the lesser the education and the lesser will be the environmental problems. Further the analysis was also made to study the relationship in detail. The findings presented in the Table–24 also shows that the monitors with different levels of education do not differ significantly on majority of the items (5 of the 6 items). However, they deffer significantly on one item namely motivating the neo-literates for continuing on one item namely motivating the neo-literates for continuing education. The trend of the obtained mean problem score of the three groups of the monitors shows that the monitors with moderate level of education felt it as a prominent problem. Keeping in the view of the above, the stated hypothesis " There is no significant difference in each problem and problem faced by JCK monitor the area of environment of JCK activities due to variations in their educational status" is accepted except in case of the item motivating the neo-literates for continuing education.

Table–23 : Mean and Standard Deviation Problem Scores of both Experience groups of JCK Monitors on each Item under the Area of 'Environment' and the calculated 't' values.

Sl.No.	Nature of the Problem	Experience				Calculated 't' values
		Less (N=56)		More (N=64)		
		Mean	S.D	Mean	S.D.	
1.	Lack of audio-visual aids to dissiminate the information to the learners in JCK	3.11	1.45	2.55	1.47	2.10*
2.	Ability to maintain hormonious relationship with the villagers.	2.96	1.45	3.08	1.38	0.43@
3.	Lack of equal participation on the part of men and women in the activities of JCK	2.82	1.42	2.78	1.61	0.14@
4.	The standard of language in the available reading materials in JCK is higher than the learners' standard.	3.16	1.36	3.50	1.41	1.33@
5.	Ability to motivate the Neo-literates for continuing education.	3.04	1.44	3.36	1.52	1.19@
6.	Choosing a suitable place for effective learning.	2.89	1.35	3.33	1.39	1.73@
Problem as a whole		17.91	4.11	18.66	5.03	0.89@

Note : * Significant at 0.05 level.
@ Not significant at 0.05 level.

Table–24: Mean and Standard Deviation Problem Scores of different Educational groups of JCK Monitors on each Item under the Area of 'Environment and the calculated 'f' values.

Sl.No.	Nature of the Problem	Education						Calculated 'f' values
		Low (N=20)		Middle (N=77)		More (N=23)		
		Mean	S.D	Mean	S.D.	Mean	S.D.	
1.	Lack of audio-visual aids to disseminate the information to the learners in JCK	2.85	1.39	2.90	1.51	2.48	1.44	0.70@
2.	Ability to maintain hormonious relationship with the villagers.	3.05	1.36	3.00	1.43	3.09	1.41	0.03@
3.	Lack of equal participation on the part of men and women in the activities of JCK	2.55	1.50	2.81	1.57	3.00	1.32	0.46@
4.	The standard of language in the available reading materials in JCK is higher than the learners' standard.	2.95	1.36	3.39	1.43	3.52	1.25	1.01@
5.	Ability to motivate the Neo-literates for continuing education.	2.75	1.41	3.43	1.52	2.87	1.30	2.405*
6.	Choosing a suitable place for effective learning.	3.05	1.43	3.12	1.38	3.22	1.38	0.80@
	Problem as a whole	17.20	4.09	18.64	4.83	18.17	4.26	0.76@

Note : * Significant at 0.05 level.
@ Not significant at 0.05 level.

The Influence of the Marital Status of the JCK Monitors on their Environmental Problems in the Organisation of JCK Activities

In order to identify the influence of the marital status of the monitors on their problems in the area of environment, the collected data were analysed area wise and itemwise in particular. The obtained results were presented in Table–25.

The above table clearly demonstrate that the mean difference of the two groups *viz.*, married and unmarried were not significantly different both in the area as a whole and also on all the items in particular. In otherwords, monitor belonging to married and unmarried groups do not differ significantly from each other on their problems in the area of environment. In view of the above results the hypothesis " There is no significant difference in each problem and problem as a whole faced by JCK monitor under the area Environment of JCK activities due to variations in their Marital Status" is accepted.

The Influence of the Personal Characteristics of the Monitors on their Problems in the Area of Co-operation

Under the area of co-operation, out of 38 items 6 items were coming under this area. The criterian of mean ± ½ S.D. was used to classify the problems into prominent, moderate and less prominent problems. As per this criteria the item–reinduction of dropouts into the school is a prominent problem, three items *viz.* obtaining co-operation from experts and officials of developmental programmes, in-adequate training for the monitors in the effective implementation of JCK and inadequate availability of books relevant to the learners interest were found to be moderate problems in this area. On the otherhand, regarding the items–lack of recognition to the monitors on par with social workers, JCKS' inability to provide training in suitable occupational skills to the women are falling under the category of less prominent problems. Hence, the programme organisers should take not of the prominent and moderate problems and should be given priority to solve these problems.

In order to findout the difference in the problems both in area as a whole and the specific items in the area among the monitors belonging to different groups a detailed analysis was done and presented in the form of tables.

Table–25: Mean and Standard Deviation Problem Scores of both Marital Status groups of JCK Monitors on each Item under the Area of 'Environment' and the calculated 't' values.

Sl.No.	Nature of the Problem	Marital Status				Calculated 't' values
		Married		Unmarried		
		Mean	S.D	Mean	S.D.	
1.	Lack of audio-visual aids to dissiminate the information to the learners in JCK	2.94	1.46	2.67	1.50	0.99@
2.	Ability to maintain hormonious relationship with the villagers.	3.06	1.37	2.98	1.47	0.31@
3.	Lack of equal participation on the part of men and women in the activities of JCK	2.84	1.42	2.75	1.63	0.31@
4.	The standard of language in the available reading materials in JCK is higher than the learners' standard.	3.33	1.38	3.35	1.42	0.68@
5.	Ability to motivate the Neo-literates for continuing education.	3.29	1.41	3.12	1.58	0.59@
6.	Choosing a suitable place for effective learning.	3.10	1.44	3.16	1.32	0.24@
Problem as a whole		18.56	4.71	18.04	4.55	0.61@

Note : * Significant at 0.05 level.
@ Not significant at 0.05 level.

Table–26: Mean and Standard Deviation Problem Scores of both sex groups of JCK Monitors on each Item under the Area of co-operation' and the calculated 't' values.

Sl.No.	Nature of the Problem	Sex				Calculated 't' values
		Men (N=60)		Women (N=60)		
		Mean	S.D	Mean	S.D.	
1.	Borrowing of good number of books by educated leaving little scope for neo- literates.	3.28	1.05	2.97	1.22	1.52@
2.	Lack of recognition to the monitors on par with social workers.	3.07	1.38	2.88	1.17	0.78@
3.	JCKs' inability to provide training in suitable occupational skills to women due to lack of co-operation from developmental departments.	2.97	1.53	3.08	1.28	0.45@
4.	Inadequate training for the Monitors for effective implementation of JCK	3.20	1.26	1.43	1.26	1.01@
5.	Reinduction of drop-outs into the schools.	3.27	1.45	3.73	1.46	1.75@
6.	Obtaining co-operation from experts and officials of developmental departments.	3.78	1.25	4.08	1.08	1.40@
Problem as a whole		19.27	4.84	19.30	3.87	0.04@

Note: * Significant at 0.05 level.
@ Note significant at 0.05 level.

The Influence of Sex of Monitors on the Problem area of Elicitation of Co-operation for Organisation of JCK Activites

From the Table–26, it is clear that men and women monitors do not differ significantly with each other, as the obtained mean differences is very small. In otherwords, men and women monitors are facing similar problems in the area of co-operation. Hence, further item analysis was also done to identify whether there were any differences between the men and women monitors on different specific problems included in the area of co-operation.

The Influence of the Caste of the JCK Monitors on their problems in the Area of Co-operation

The difference between the mean problem score of the S.C./ S.T, B.C and F.C monitors in the area of co-operation are shown in Table– 27.

The table clearly demonstrate that the three groups of monitors do not differ in their problems in the area co-operation as a whole. The obtained mean problem scores of these three groups in the area indicate that the S.C./S.T monitors have experienced more problems in elicitation of co-operation from different sources followed by S.C. and.B.C monitors.

The itemwise analysis presented in the table also discloses that the mean differences of the three groups on all the items were not significant. In otherwords, all the three groups of monitors have similar problems in elicitation of co-operation from different sources. In view of the above results, the stated hypothesis "There is no significant difference in each problem and problem as a whole faced by JCK Monitors under the area of Co-operation of JCK activities due to variations in their caste" is accepted with respect to the area as a whole as well as specific items under the area.

Influence of Monitors' Occupation on their Problems in the Area of Co-operation

From the table 28, it is evident that the difference between the mean problem score obtained by the monitors with different occupational backgrounds do not differ significantly. In otherwords,

Table–27: Mean and Standard Deviation Problem Scores of different caste groups of JCK Monitors on each Item under the Area of Co-operation' and the calculated 'f' values.

Sl.No.	Nature of the Problem	Caste						Calculated 'f' values
		S.C/S/T (N=38)		B.C. (N=43)		F.C. (N=39)		
		Mean	S.D	Mean	S.D.	Mean	S.D.	
1.	Borrowing of good number of books by educated leaving little scope for neo literates.	3.32	1.13	2.98	1.17	3.10	1.13	0.87@
2.	Lack of recognition to the monitors on par with social workers.	3.11	1.31	2.95	1.33	2.87	1.18	0.32@
3.	JCKs' in ability to provide training in suitable occupational skills to women due to lack of co-operation from developmental departments.	3.24	1.44	3.07	1.44	2.77	1.31	1.08@
4.	Inadequate training for the Monitors for effective implementation of JCK	3.34	1.34	3.12	1.22	3.51	1.20	1.00@
5.	Reinduction of drop-outs into the schools.	3.53	1.52	3.28	1.48	3.72	1.38	0.90@
6.	Obtaining co-operation from experts and officials of developmental departments.	3.87	1.10	3.86	1.36	4.08	1.02	0.42@
Problem as a whole		19.97	4.55	18.53	4.60	19.44	3.80	1.11@

Note : * Significant at 0.05 level.
@ Not significant at 0.05 level

Table–28 : Mean and Standard Deviation problem Scores of different Occupational groups of JCK Monitors on each Item under the Area of 'Co-operation' and the calculated 'f' values.

Sl.No.	Nature of the Problem	Occupation						Calculated 'f' values
		Agriculture (N=75)		Coolie (N=20)		Others (N=25)		
		Mean	S.D	Mean	S.D.	Mean	S.D.	
1.	Borrowing of good number of books by educated leaving little scope for neo-literates.	3.07	1.15	3.65	1.19	2.88	0.99	2.80*
2.	Lack of recognition to the monitors on par with social workers.	2.97	1.22	3.10	1.41	2.88	1.34	0.16@
3.	JCKs' inability to provide training in suitable occupational skills to women due to lack of co-operation from developmental departments.	2.75	1.35	3.65	1.31	3.36	1.44	4.31*
4.	Inadequate training for the Monitors for effective implementation of JCK	3.23	1.33	3.55	1.24	3.40	1.02	0.57@
5.	Reinduction of drop-outs into the schools.	3.31	1.53	3.65	1.35	3.96	1.25	1.98*
6.	Obtaining co-operation from experts and officials of developmental departments.	3.83	1.81	4.00	1.14	4.20	1.13	0.96@
Problem as a whole		18.64	4.43	20.85	4.49	19.96	3.68	2.42*

Note: * Significant at 0.05 level.
@ Not significant at 0.05 level.

the occupational background of the monitors does not have any influence on their problems in the area of co-operation.

The itemwise analysis of the problems in the area of co-operation shown in Table–28 also indicate that the three groups differ significantly on two items only inadequate availability of books relevant to the interest of learners and JCKs' inability to provide training in suitable occupational skills to the women. The trend of the obtained mean problem scores of the monitors shows that the monitors with wage earning and labourering monitors considered the above problems as prominent problems. The three groups of monitors do not differ significantly on the rest of the items. In view of the above results, the stated hypothesis, "There is no significant difference in each problem and problem as a whole faced by JCK monitor under the area of co-operation of JCK activities due to variations in their occupation" is accepted in case of the area as a whole and rejected in case of the two items –inadequate availability of the books relevant to the interest of the learners and JCKs inability to provide training in suitable occupational skills to women.

Influence of JCK Monitors Income on their problems in the Area of Co-operation

The result presented in the Table–29 shows that the monitors with less, moderate and more income groups do not differ significantly with each other in their problems in the area of co-operation as the calculated 'F- value is less than the table value. However, the mean differences show that the moderate income group of monitors experience more problems in the area followed by less and more income group monitors.

The itemwise analysis shown in the table clearly indicates that the monitors of these groups do not differ significantly on any of the six items. In otherwords, the monitors of these three groups have similar problems in the area of co-operation. In view of the above results, the stated hypothesis " There is no significant difference in each problem and problem as a whole faced by JCK monitor under the area of co-operation of JCK activities due to variations in their income" is accepted both in case of the area as a whole and the items cited.

Table–29 : Mean and Standard Deviation Problem Scores of income groups of JCK Monitors on each Item under the Area of 'Co-operation' and the calculated 'f' values.

Sl.No.	Nature of the Problem	Income						Calculated 'f' values
		Low (N=30)		Middle (N=57)		More (N=39)		
		Mean	S.D	Mean	S.D.	Mean	S.D.	
1.	Borrowing of good number of books by educated leaving little scope for neo-literates.	3.47	0.88	2.92	1.22	3.13	1.18	2.13*
2.	Lack of recognition to the monitors on par with social workers.	3.10	1.27	3.00	1.20	2.85	1.37	0.32@
3.	JCK's inability to provide training in suitable occupational skills to women due to lack of co-operation from developmental departments.	3.07	1.34	3.27	1.39	2.67	1.42	2.08*
4.	Inadequate training to the Monitors for effective implementation of JCK	3.07	1.34	3.25	1.22	3.59	1.21	1.55@
5.	Lack of Co-operation from the schools for reinduction of dropout children	3.57	1.36	3.53	1.56	3.41	1.43	0.11@
6.	Obtaining co-operation from experts and officials of developmental departments.	3.97	1.08	4.06	1.11	3.74	1.31	0.79@
Problem as a whole		19.47	3.51	19.57	4.93	30.87	5.00	0.39@

Note: * Significant at 0.05 level.
@ Not significant at 0.05 level.

Table–30: Mean and Standard Deviation Problem Scores of both Experience groups of JCK Monitors on each Item under the Area of 'Co-operation' and the calculated 't' values.

Sl.No.	Nature of the Problem	Experience				Calculated 'f' values
		Less (N=56)		More (N=64)		
		Mean	S.D	Mean	S.D.	
1.	Borrowing of good number of books by educated leaving little scope for neo-literates.	3.07	1.05	3.17	1.23	0.48@
2.	Lack of recognition to the monitors on par with social workers.	2.77	1.25	3.16	1.28	1.67@
3.	JCKs' inability to provide training in suitable occupational skills to women due to lack of co-operation from developmental departments.	2.88	1.30	3.16	1.49	1.10@
4.	Inadequate training to the Monitors for effective implementation of JCK	3.25	1.11	3.38	1.39	0.54@
5.	Lack of Co-operation from the schools for reinduction of dropout children.	3.38	1.46	3.61	1.47	0.87@
6.	Obtaining co-operation from experts and officials of developmental departments.	3.91	1.12	3.95	1.23	0.19@
Problem as a whole		18.52	3.76	19.95	4.76	1.84@

Note: * Significant at 0.05 level.
@ Not significant at 0.05 level.

Influence of the Experience of the JCK Monitors on their Problems in the Area of Co-operation

The result presented in the Table–30 shows that the monitors with less and more experienced groups do not differ significantly from each other in their problems in the area of co-operation. However, the mean difference of 1.43 points reveals that more experienced monitors considered the area as the more problematic than less experienced monitors.

The results presented in the table discloses that monitors from less and more experienced group do not differ significantly with each other on any of the 6 items listed under the area. It appears that both categories of the monitors have similar problems. In view of the above, the hypothesis " There is no significant difference in each problem and problem as a whole faced by JCK monitors under the area co-operation of JCK activities due to variations in their Experience" is accepted both in case of area as a whole and the items in particular.

Influence of the Educational Status of the JCK Monitors on their Problems in the Area of Co-operation

Table–31 shows the mean and S.D scores of the monitors belonging to low, moderate and more income groups.

In Table–31, the three groups do not differ significantly from each other. However, the trend of the mean problem scores shows that the monitors with more educational background considered the area as more problematic followed by the monitors with moderate and low level of education.

The results presented in Table–31 also indicates the monitors with three levels of education does not differ significantly from each other. From the above, it appears that the monitors with three levels of education are facing similar problems. In view of the above, the stated hypothesis " There is no significant difference in each problem and problem as a whole faced by JCK monitor under the area of co-operation of JCK activities due to variations in their Educational Status" is accepted.

Table–31: Mean and Standard Deviation Problem Scores of different Education groups of JCK Monitors on each Item under the Area of 'Co-operation' and the calculated 'f' values.

Sl.No.	Nature of the Problem	Education						Calculated 'f' values
		Low (N=20)		Middle (N=77)		More (N=23)		
		Mean	S.D	Mean	S.D.	Mean	S.D.	
1.	Borrowing of good number of books by educated leaving little scope for neo-literates.	3.40	1.20	3.05	1.12	3.13	1.19	0.71@
2.	Lack of recognition to the monitors on par with social workers.	2.95	1.36	2.94	1.22	3.13	1.39	0.20@
3.	JCKs' inability to provide training in suitable occupational skills to women due to lack of co-operation from developmental departments.	2.55	1.43	3.21	1.39	2.83	1.34	2.02*
4.	Inadequate training to the Monitors for effective implementation of JCK	3.50	1.24	3.26	1.27	3.35	1.24	0.28@
5.	Lack of Co-operation from experts and officials of developmental departments.	3.52	1.20	4.01	1.21	4.09	0.93	2.06*
Problem as a whole		18.45	3.46	19.40	4.62	19.61	4.18	0.44@

Note: * Significant at 0.05 level.
@ Not significant at 0.05 level.

Influence of the Marital Status of the JCk Monitors on their Problems in the area of Co-operation

The results presented in the Table–32 clearly show that the monitors belonging to the married and unmarried groups do not differ significantly from each other as the mean differences is very less. In other words, both the groups possess similar problems in the area of co-operation.

The result presented in the Table–32 indicates that the two groups of monitors do not differ significantly from each other on any of the items listed under the area 'co-operation. In otherwords, marital status does not have any influence on the area of co-operation. In view of the above results, the hypothesis " There is no significant difference in each problem and problem as a whole faced by JCK monitor under the area co-operation of JCK activities due to variations in their marital status" is accepted both in the case of area problem and the problems in particular.

Influence of the Personal Characteristics of the JCK Monitors on their Problems relating to the Materials

In order to identify the problems of the monitors in the area of materials, a list of 8 items were prepared and presented to the monitors with a request to rate the problems according to their experience. Further, the influence of the characteristics of the monitors on their problems in the area of materials was also studied.

The analysis of the mean problem scores obtained for all the items in the area of materials shows that the mean problems score of the area is 3.55. The mean of the area clearly shows that the monitors have rated it as their priority problem area. In order to identify the priority items in the area, the items were categorised into three groups based on the criteria, mean ± ½ S.D. According to this criteria six items were found to be prominent problems and one each belongs to moderate and less prominent problem respectively. The prominent problems identified in this area on getting return of the books from borrowers, lack of suitable place for organisation of sports and games, lack of regular supply of newspapers to JCKs, organisation of activities in all affiliated hamlets of the JCKs, and organising need based activities in the JCKs. The items–lack of training and experience

Table–32 : Mean and Standard Deviation Problem Scores of both Marital Status groups of JCK Monitors on each Item under the Area of 'Co-operation' and the calculated 't' values.

Sl.No.	Nature of the Problem	Marital Status				Calculated 'f' values
		Married (N=63)		Unmarried (N=57)		
		Mean	S.D	Mean	S.D.	
1.	Borrowing of good number of books by educated leaving little scope for neo-literates.	3.02	1.12	3.25	1.17	1.09@
2.	Lack of recognition to the monitors on par with social workers.	2.86	1.26	3.11	1.29	1.06@
3.	JCKs' inability to provide training in suitable occupational skills to women due to lack of co-operation from developmental departments.	2.90	1.42	3.16	1.39	0.98@
4.	Inadequate training to the Monitors for effective implementation of JCK	3.41	1.15	3.21	1.37	0.87@
5.	Lack of Co-operation from the schools for reinduction of dropout children.	3.43	1.48	3.58	1.46	0.56@
6.	Obtaining co-operation from experts and officials of developmental departments.	3.87	1.23	4.00	1.12	0.59@
Problem as a whole		18.95	4.41	19.65	4.32	0.87@

Note: * Significant at 0.05 level.
@ Not significant at 0.05 level.

among the monitors for conducting cultural programmes and lack of motivation among communities to participate in Charcha Mandals were also rated as moderate and less prominent problems respectively.

Influence of the Sex of the Monitor on their Problems in the Area of Materials

The result presented in Table–33 shows that the mean problem score difference between men and women monitors are not significant. However, the trend of the obtained mean problem score shows that women monitors are of the opinion that the area is more problematic for them.

The findings of itemwise analysis presented in the table 33 clearly shows that men and women monitors differ significantly in their mean problem scores only on one item *i.e.*, organising need based activities in the JCK In otherwords, they agree with each other on majority of the problems (seven out of eight). However, the obtained mean problem scores on the above item showed that women monitors rated it as a prominent problem. In view of the above results the hypothesis " There is no significant difference in each problem and problem as a whole faced by JCK monitor under the area Material of JCK activities due to variations in their Sex" is accepted except in case of the item organising need based activities in JCK.

Influence of the Caste of the Monitors on their Problems in the Area of Materials

The results presented in the Table–34 reveals that the monitors belonging to S.C./S.T. , B.C. and F.C. groups differ significantly in their mean problem scores. The obtained mean problem scores reveals that monitors with F.C. background rated it as prominent problem and B.C. and S.C., S.T. monitors rate almost similarly with less intensity.

From the above table it is also evident that the monitors with different caste groups differ significantly with each other on 3 of the 8 items in area. The trend of the obtained mean in problem scores clearly shows that F.C. group has rated all the items (getting return of the Library books from borrowers, organisation of activities in all affiliated hamlets of the JCK and organising need based activities in

Table–33: Mean and Standard Deviation Problem Scores of both Sex groups of JCK Monitors on each Item under the Area of 'Material' and the calculated 't' values.

Sl.No.	Nature of the Problem	Sex				Calculated 't' values
		Men (N=60)		Women (N=60)		
		Mean	S.D	Mean	S.D.	
1.	Getting return of the books from borrowers.	3.52	1.45	3.70	1.36	0.71@
2.	Lack of training and suitable materials to the Monitors for conducting cultural programmes.	3.00	1.48	3.67	1.43	2.50*
3.	Lack of suitable infrastructure for the organisation of Sports and Games.	3.88	1.37	3.75	1.34	0.54@
4.	Irregular supply of Newspapers to JCK.	3.43	1.45	3.55	1.27	0.46@
5.	Lack of suitable materials to motivate the community to participate in Charcha Mandals.	3.08	1.37	2.97	1.24	0.48@
6.	Lack of adequate facilities in the organisation of activities in all affiliated hamlets of the JCK	3.55	1.32	3.77	1.61	0.80@
7.	Lack of adequate lighting facilities in JCK	3.55	1.36	3.62	1.13	0.29@
8.	Lack of suitable materials in organising need based activities.	3.65	1.55	4.18	1.02	2.22*
	Problem as a whole	27.67	6.74	29.20	4.77	1.33@

Note: * Significant at 0.05 level.
@ Not significant at 0.05 level.

Table–34 : Mean and Standard Deviation problem Scores of different caste groups of JCK Monitors on each Item under the Area of 'Material' and the calculated 'f' values.

Sl.No.	Nature of the Problem	Caste						Calculated 'f' values
		S.C/S/T (N=38)		B.C. (N=43)		F.C. (N=39)		
		Mean	S.D	Mean	S.D.	Mean	S.D.	
1.	Getting return of the books from borrowers.	3.45	1.43	3.37	1.51	4.03	1.17	2.60*
2.	Lack of training and suitable materials to the Monitors for conducting cultural programmes.	3.05	1.49	3.30	1.46	3.64	1.49	1.50@
3.	Lack of suitable infrastructure for the organisation of Sports and Games.	3.74	1.35	3.79	1.30	3.92	1.40	0.19@
4.	Irregular supply of Newspapers to JCK.	3.29	1.57	3.51	1.32	3.67	1.16	0.73@
5.	Lack of suitable materials to motivate the community to participate in charchamandals.	3.11	1.29	2.88	1.33	3.10	1.28	0.38@
6.	Lack of adequate facilities in the organisation of activities in all affiliated hamlets of the JCK	3.42	1.44	3.47	1.56	4.10	1.30	2.68*
7.	Lack of adequate lighting facilities in JCK	3.61	1.29	3.72	1.19	3.41	1.26	0.63@
8.	Lack of suitable materials organising need based activities.	3.71	1.49	3.63	1.43	4.44	0.84	4.60*
Problem as a whole		27.37	6.41	27.67	6.26	30.31	5.88	2.60*

Note: * Significant at 0.05 level.
@ Not significant at 0.05 level.

the JCK are as more prominent problems. However, the three caste groups does not differ significantly from each other on the rest of the items. In view of the above results the hypothesis, "There is no significant difference in each problem and problem as a whole faced by JCk monitor under the area Material of JCK activities due to variations in their caste" is accepted except in case of above three items only.

Influence of the Occupation of the Monitors on their Problems in the Area of Materials

Influence of the occupation of the monitors on their problems in the area of materials are as shown in the Table–35.

The table reveals that the monitors with different occupational groups do not differ significantly with each other. The further analysis in terms of item analysis shows that the three occupational groups of monitors do not differ significantly from each other on all the items listed under the area. In view of the above the hypothesis " There is no significant difference in each problem and problem as a whole faced by JCK monitor under the area Material of JCK activities due to variations in their occupation" is accepted.

Influence of the Income of the Monitors on their Problems in the Area of Materials

The result presented in the Table–36 shows that the monitors with less moderate and more income groups do no significantly differ from each other on the problem area materials. However, the mean problem scores show that the monitors with moderate income group have stated it as a more prominent problem area followed by the monitors with more and less income groups.

The result of itemwise analysis presented in the Table–36 shows that the monitors with less, moderate and more income groups differ significantly only on one item *i.e.* organisation of activities in all affiliated hamlets of the JCK. The mean problem scores show that moderate income group has rated it as more prominent problem followed by more and less income groups. In view of the above the hypothesis " There is no significant difference in each problem and

Table–35 : Mean and Standard Deviation Problem Scores of different occupation groups of JCK Monitors on each Item under the Area of Material, and the calculated 'f' values.

Sl.No.	Nature of the Problem	Occupation						Calculated 'f' values
		Agriculture (N=75)		Coolie (N=20)		Others (N=25)		
		Mean	S.D	Mean	S.D.	Mean	S.D.	
1.	Getting return of the books from borrowers.	3.68	1.42	3.30	1.45	3.64	1.32	0.57@
2.	Lack of training and suitable materials to the Monitors for conducting cultural programmes.	3.33	1.52	3.00	1.45	3.60	1.41	0.88@
3.	Lack of suitable infrastructure for the organisation of sports and Games.	3.81	1.33	4.05	1.16	3.60	1.41	0.88@
4.	Irregular supply of Newspapers to JCK.	3.44	1.37	3.80	1.54	3.88	1.11	1.52@
5.	Lack of suitable materials to motivate the community to participate in Charchamandals.	3.04	1.29	3.30	1.42	2.76	1.21	0.95@
6.	Lack of adequate facilities in the organisation of activities in all affiliated hamlets of the JCK	3.77	1.41	3.75	1.34	3.24	1.68	1.26@
7.	Lack of adequate lighting facilities in JCK	3.51	1.25	3.85	1.24	3.60	1.23	0.59@
8.	Lack of suitable materials in organising need based activities	3.92	1.37	3.55	1.43	4.20	1.06	1.30@
	Problem as a whole	28.51	6.37	28.00	6.45	28.56	6.07	0.05@

Note: * Significant at 0.05 level.
@ Not significant at 0.05 level.

Table–36 : Mean and Standard Deviation Problem Scores of different Income groups of JCK Monitors on each Item under the Area of 'Material' and the calculated 'f' values.

Sl.No.	Nature of the Problem	Income						Calculated 'f' values
		Low (N=30)		Middle (N=57)		More (N=39)		
		Mean	S.D	Mean	S.D.	Mean	S.D.	
1.	Getting return of the books from borrowers.	3.30	1.53	3.84	1.18	3.54	1.53	1.47@
2.	Lack of training and suitable materials to the Monitors for conducting cultural programmes.	3.10	1.40	3.35	1.56	3.49	1.47	0.56@
3.	Lack of suitable infrastructure for the organisation of Sports and Games.	4.00	1.18	3.82	1.46	3.67	1.31	0.50@
4.	Irregular supply of Newspapers to JCK.	3.27	1.41	3.55	1.35	3.59	1.33	0.54@
5.	Lack of suitable materials to motivate the community to participate in Charchamandals.	2.97	1.11	3.31	1.35	2.69	1.30	2.58*
6.	Lack of adequate facilities in the organisation of activities in all affiliated hamlets of the JCk	2.87	1.71	4.14	1.28	3.64	1.23	7.74*
7.	Lack of adequate lighting facilities in JCK	3.67	1.16	3.51	1.35	3.62	1.17	0.16@
8.	Lack of suitable materials in organising need based activities.	3.67	1.25	4.08	1.27	3.90	1.46	0.89@
	Problem as a whole	26.43	6.93	29.61	5.94 2	8.44	5.92	2.41*

Note : * Significant at 0.05 level.
@ Not significant at 0.05 level.

problem as a whole faced by JCK monitor under the area Material of JCK activities due to variations in their Income" is accepted in case of the area as a whole and items in particular except in case of the item organisation of activities in all affiliated hamlets of the JCK.

Influence of the Experience of the Monitors on their Problems in the Area of Material

The Table–37 reveals that the monitors do not differ significantly from each other on the problem area of materials as a whole. In addition to the above, the results relating to the itemwise analysis presented in the table also supports the above finding as these two groups do not differ on any of the items listed in the area. In the view of the above the hypothesis " There is no significant difference in each problem and problem as a whole faced by JCK monitor under the area material of JCK activities due to variations in their experience" is accepted both in terms of area as a whole and on all items in particular.

Influence of the Educational Status of the Monitors in their Problems in the Area of Materials.

The analysis of the results relating to the influence of level of education of the monitors on their problems in the area of materials is presented in Table–38.

The table shows that the monitors with three levels of education differ significantly with each other. The trend of the mean problem scores discloses that the monitors with more level of education have stated it as a more prominent problem area for them followed by the monitors with moderate and low level of education. The itemwise analysis presented in the table also indicates that the monitors belonging to the three groups differ significantly on items getting return of the books from borrowers, lack of training and experience among the monitors for conducting cultural programmes and organising need based activities in the JCK. The trend of the mean problem scores of the above three items discloses that the monitors with more level of education have rated the above items as more prominent problems followed by monitors with moderate and low level of education. In view of the findings, the hypothiesis " There is no significant difference in each problem and problem as a whole faced

Table–37 : Mean and Standard Deviation Problem Scores of both experience groups of JCK Monitors on each Item under the Area of 'Material' and the calculated 't' values.

Sl.No.	Nature of the Problem	Experience				Calculated 't' values
		Less (N=56)		More (N=64)		
		Mean	S.D	Mean	S.D.	
1.	Getting return of the books from borrowers.	3.73	1.29	3.50	1.50	0.91@
2.	Lack of training and suitable materials to the Monitors for conducting cultural programmes.	3.34	1.37	3.33	1.60	0.04@
3.	Lack of suitable infrastructure for the organisation of Sports and Games.	3.80	1.32	3.83	1.39	0.09@
4.	Irregular supply of Newspapers to JCK.	3.34	1.34	3.63	1.28	1.15@
5.	Lack of suitable materials to motivate the community to participate in Charcha Mandals.	3.09	1.23	2.97	1.37	0.50@
6.	Lack of adequate facilities in the organisation of activities in all affiliated hamlets of the JCK	3.48	1.54	3.81	1.40	1.22@
7.	Lack of adequate lighting facilities in JCK	3.66	1.14	3.52	1.33	0.64@
8.	Lack of suitable materials in organising need based activities.	3.98	1.17	3.86	1.47	0.50@
Problem as a whole		28.32	5.90	28.52	6.67	0.183@

Note : * Significant at 0.05 level.
@ Not significant at 0.05 level.

Table–38 : Mean and Standard Deviation Problem Scores of different Education groups of JCK Monitors on each Item under the Area of 'Material' and the calculated 'f' values.

Sl.No.	Nature of the Problem	Education						Calculated 'f' values
		Low (N=20)		Middle (N=77)		More (N=23)		
		Mean	S.D	Mean	S.D.	Mean	S.D.	
1.	Getting return of the books from borrowers.	2.95	1.56	3.71	1.27	3.83	1.55	2.72*
2.	Lack of training and suitable materials to the Monitors for conducting cultural programmes.	2.90	1.41	3.30	1.52	3.83	1.34	2.12*
3.	Lack of suitable infrastructure for the organisation of Sports and Games.	3.70	1.19	3.79	1.42	4.00	1.25	0.29@
4.	Irregular supply of Newspapers to JCK.	3.80	1.47	3.52	1.33	3.65	1.34	0.62@
5.	Lack of suitable materials to motivate the community to participate in Charcha Mandals.	2.85	1.35	3.12	1.26	2.87	1.39	0.52@
6.	Lack of adequate facilities in the organisation of activities in all affiliated hamlets of the JCK	3.55	1.40	3.55	1.57	4.13	1.08	1.45@
7.	Lack of adequate lighting facilities	3.30	1.23	3.60	1.29	3.78	1.06	0.80@
8.	Lack of suitable materials in organising need based activities.	3.55	1.46	4.00	1.30	4.13	1.23	2.26*
	Problem as a whole	25.80	5.90	28.58	6.25	30.20	6.19	2.72*

Note : * Significant at 0.05 level.
@ Not significant at 0.05 level.

Table 39: Mean and Standard Deviation Problem Scores of both Marital Status groups of JCK Monitors on each Item under the Area of 'Material' and the calculated 't' values.

Sl.No.	Nature of the Problem	Marital Status				Calculated 'f' values
		Married (N=63)		Unmarried (N=57)		
		Mean	S.D	Mean	S.D.	
1.	Getting return of the books from borrowers.	3.78	1.31	3.43	1.49	1.38@
2.	Lack of training and suitable materials to the Monitors for conducting cultural programmes.	3.56	1.47	3.09	1.49	1.73@
3.	Lack of suitable infrastructure for the organisation of Sports and Games.	3.75	1.43	3.89	1.27	0.60@
4.	Irregular supply of Newspapers to JCK.	3.59	1.43	3.89	1.27	0.79@
5.	Lack of suitable materials to motivate the community to participate in Charchamandals.	2.86	1.31	3.21	1.28	1.49@
6.	Lack of adequate facilities in the organisation of activities in all affiliated hamlets of the JCK	3.84	1.36	3.46	1.57	1.43@
7.	Lack of adequate lighting facilities in JCK	3.51	1.26	3.67	1.23	0.69@
8.	Lack of suitable materials in organising need based activities	4.11	1.20	2.70	1.45	1.67@
Problem as a whole		28.98	5.40	27.82	7.16	0.99@

Note : * Significant at 0.5 level.
@ Not significant at 0.05 level.

by JCK monitor under the area Material of JCK activities due to variations in their Educational Status" is accepted in case of the above three items only.

Influence of the Marital Status of the Monitors on their Problems in the Area of Material

The analysis of the data relating to the study of influence of the marital status of the monitor on their problems in the area of materials were presented in Table–39.

The findings presented in the above table states that the married and un married monitors do not differ significantly with each other in respect of the problem area 'materials' as a whole and the items in particular. In view of the above results, the stated hypothesis "There is no significant difference in problem and problem as a whole faced by JCK monitor under the area materials of JCK activities due to variations in their marital status" is accepted in terms of area as well as the items in particular.

SUMMARY AND CONCLUSIONS

INTRODUCTION

Recognising the relationship between literacy and socio economic development, the government of India has launched a number of Adult Education Programmes for the promotion of literacy. The current Adult Education programmes are being organised under N.L.M. The aim of the N.L.M. is to eradicate illiteracy among 100 million Adults in the age group of 15 to 35 years. In order to encourage mass participation and voluntarism in eradication of illiteracy, the campaign approach was adopted. As a test case for total literacy, Ernakulam literacy project was sanctioned. The success of campaign paved a way for launching 10 total literacy campaign through out the country. Chittor district Total Literacy campaign was one among them. The successful implementation of T.L.C. at Chittoor has created a new situation of emergence of millions of Neo-literates.

In order to retain the literacy, promotion of literacy, consolidation of literacy, post literacy and continuing education programme is being implemented in the form of *Jan Chaithanaya Kendras* in the district. There are 10,000 JCKs functioning in the district. Each JCK is manned by a monitor. The functions of the monitor are as follows: Motivating learners to attend JCK, supply same. The specific objectives of the study are as follows.

Objectives of the Study

The objectives of the study are

1. To identify the problems of monitors in organising the JCKs.
2. To findout the relationship between the personal traits and problems of the monitors.

3. To find out the differences if any, in the intensity of the problems faced by the Monitors due to variations in their sex, caste, occupation, income, experience, education and maritala status.

In the lite of the above objectives the following hypothesis were formulated for testing.

Hypothesis of the Study

The Hypothesis of the study are as follows:

1. There is no significant association between the personal traits (sex, caste, occupation, income, experience, education and marital status) and the problems faced by the JCK monitors.
2. There is no significant difference in each problem and problems as a whole faced by JCK monitors in the area 'Organisation' of JCK activities due to variations in their sex, caste, occupation, income, experience, educational status and marital status.
3. There is no significant difference in each problem and problems as a whole faced by JCK monitors in the area 'Administration' of JCK activities due to variations in their sex, caste, occupation, income, experience, educational status marital status.
4. There is no significant difference in each problem and problems as a whole faced by JCK monitors in the area 'Environment', of JCK activities due to variations in their sex, caste, occupation, income, experience, educational status and marital status.
5. There is no significant difference in each problem and problems as a whole faced by JCK monitors in the area 'C-operation' of JCK activities due to variations in their sex, caste, occupation, income, experience, educational status and marital status.
6. There is no significant difference in each problem and problems as a whole faced by JCK monitors in the area 'Material', of JCK activities due to variations in their sex, caste, occupation, income, experience, educational status and marital status.

Scope of the Study

The study is intended to identify the problems of the monitors, categorisation of problems into prominent problems, moderate problems and less prominent problems. Further, it is also aimed at studying the problems of the monitors with special reference to organisation, administration, environment, co-operation and material resources. Further the association between the personal characteristics of the monitors and prerak problems were also studied. In addition areas were also identified regarding the differences if any among the monitors due to variations in their sex, caste, occupation, income, experience, educational status and marital status.

Need and Importance of the Study

The success of KCKs, largely lies on the capacity and capabilities of the monitors in overcoming the local problems and in adopting the local environment. Further, Monitors should be in a position to identify the problems and to formulate suitable strategies to overcome them in the process of achieving the objectives of he JCKs. However, not all the Monitors were in a position to do the above due to their varied socio-economic and educational backgrounds. Hence in order to improve the efficiency of the Monitor in particular and the programme as a whole, it is necessary to identify the common problems of the working Monitors. The knowledge of the anticipated problems of the monitors may be provided to the perspective monitors through pre-service and in service training so as to formulate suitable strategies depending on the nature and extent of the problems to overcome them. Keeping in view of the above, the present study on the identification of the problems of the monitors were formulated.

Methodology

For the purpose of present study a specially designed monitors problem rating scale was utilised not only for identification of problem but also to study the intensity of the problem. The problem inventory consisted of two sections. Section one of the tool is meant to identify the personal characteristics of the monitors, section two of the tool consisted of 38 monitors; problems belonging to five broad areas viz., organisation, administration, environment, co-operation and material resources. The validity and reliability of the tool were established and found to be considerably high.

The relevant data were collected by administering the tool to the 200 monitors chosen at random. The data thus collected was analysed by using appropriate statistical technique.

Findings

The findings of the study were as follows:

1. Out of 38 problem items 12 items were found to be prominent problems and 13 of them were found to be moderate problems.

2. The association between caste and problems relating to the 'organisation' and 'co-operation' were found to be significant.

3. There are no significant between different groups of monitors due to variations in their sex, caste, occupation, income, experience, education and marital status in the area as a whole. The monitors belonging to men and women, low, moderate and more income groups and Less experienced and more experienced significantly differed from each other on the problem 'elicitation of co-operation from village leaders'. In addition to above, monitors with low, moderate and more education groups significantly differed on the items–Lack of provision for the production of posters and charts for the propagation of JCK activities, Irrelevance of the available books in JCK to the interest of adults and the JCK activities were affected by different castes and religions.

4. There is no significant difference between the monitors belonging to different groups. They did not differ significantly with each other on the problem of Administration of the JCKs as a whole. However, the monitors belonging to F.C., B.C. and S.C/S.T. differed significantly on the item. The working monitors age and experience does not suit for discussion of village problems in Charcha Mandals. The monitors with different occupations differed significantly on the item–Lack of suitable sports and games materials at the JCK. In addition to above,

the monitors with different income background also differed significantly on the item–Charcha Mandals activities were affected due to village politics and taking special care the backward learners.

5. There is significant difference between the monitors belonging to different caste and occupational groups in the problem area ' environment' as a whole. The itemwise analysis reveals that monitors belonging to different occupational and experience groups differed significantly on the item Lack of audio-visual aids to dissiminate the information to the learners in JCK. The item-Ability to motivate the Neo-literates for continuing education was found to be significantly differing among the monitors belonging to different occupational and educational groups. The monitors belonging to F.C. and B.C. and S.C./S.T. groups and experience differed significantly on the problem Lack of equal participation on the part of men and women in the activities of JCK differently. The men monitors perceived the item choosing a suitable place for effective learning as more prominent problem that the women monitors.

6. Monitors belonging to different groups perceived the problem area 'co-operation' as a whole similarly, except the monitors belonging to different occupations. The findings also revealed that the monitors belonging to different occupations differed significantly on the items–Borrowing of good number of books by educated leaving little scope for neo- literates, JCKs' in ability to provide training in suitable occupational skills to women due to lack of co-operation from developmental departments and Reinduction of drop-outs into the schools. Similarly monitors with different income groups differed significantly on the items–Borrowing of good number of books by educated leaving little scope for neo–iterates. JCKs' in ability to provide training in suitable occupational skills to women due to lack of co-operation from developmental departments. It was also found that monitors with different educational backgrounds differed significantly on the items – JCKs' inability to provide training in suitable occupational skills to women due to lack of co-operation from developmental departments.

7. The problem area of 'materials' was perceived by the monitors differently. By different groups *viz.* sex, occupation, experience and marital status groups perceived similarly. On the other hand the monitors belonging to different caste, income and educational groups felt differently. The itemwise analysis reveals that men and women monitors differed on the items- Lack of training and suitable materials to the Monitors for conducting cultural programmes. Lack of suitable materials in organising need based activities, F.F., B.C. and S.C./S.T monitors differed on Getting return of the books from borrowers. Lack of adequate facilities in the organisation of activities in all affiliated hamlets of the JCK. On the other hand, monitors with different income groups differed on the items– Lack of suitable materials to motivate the community to participate in Charcha Mandals and Lack of adequate facilities in the organisation of activities in all affiliated hamlets of the JCK. Finally, monitors with different levels of education differed on Getting return of the books from borrowers, lack of training and suitable materials to the monitors for conducting cultural programmes and lack of suitable materials in organising need based activities.

Implications of the Study

The findings of the study help in identification of the problems faced by the working monitors of J.C.Ks. The knowledge of the anticipated problems and the factors associated with them will go a long way in solving the day to day problems in organisation of J.C.Ks. This knowledge also will be helpful in restricting in the training curriculum relating to the preservice and in service training. The knowledge of the association of monitor characteristics and the problems will help programme planners to choose suitable youth as monitors for successful implementation of a programme.

Limitations of the Study

1. The present study is limited to the monitors working in Chittoor District of Rayalaseema Region in Andhra Pradesh State.
2. The study is limited to find out the problems of the monitors only in organising JCKs.

3. The personal factors of the monitors such as sex, caste, occupation, income, experience, education and marital status are only chosen for analysing their association with the problems.
4. The study has involved only 200 monitors.
5. To identify the problems and their intensity, the rating scale is the only tool used.

SUGGESTIONS FOR THE FURTHER RESEARCH

1. A similar study with more sample covering different geographical areas may be undertaken.
2. An investigation to identify the anticipation of the problems experienced by the monitors and to generate suitable strategies to overcome may be undertaken.
3. A study to identify the impact of the problems on monitor effectiveness may be undertaken.
4. A study to find out the factors associated with the monitors problem may be conducted.

BIBLIOGRAPHY

Adilakshmi (1993) : An Investigation into the working conditions of the Jana Shikshana Nilayams and 'Opinion' towards Jana Sikshana Nilayams. Master Dissertation, S.P. Mahila University.

Desh Pannde (1993): Evaluation of Literacy Campaign of Jalna, Pune: Indian Institute of Education.

Denzin Saldana (1992): Evaluation of Literacy Campaign, Wardha, Bombay: Tata Institute of Social Sciences.

Directorate of Adult Education (ORG) (1994): An Evaluation of the functioning of the scheme of JSN's, New Delhi: Directorate of Adult Education, Govt. of India.

Krishna Murthy (1992) Evaluation of Literacy Campaign, Chittoor District, Andhra Pradesh, Hyderaba, University of Hyderabad.

Kumara Swamy, T. and Padmanabhaiah (1995): " An identification of the problems faced by the monitors, Indian" Journal of Adult Education, Vol. 56 (2), April - June PP - 42-46.

Mishra, R.R. (1994): Evaluation of Literacy Campaign, Ratlam, Ujjain: Vikram University (Centre for Adult Continuing Education and Extension).

Mushtaq Ahmed (1994): "Evaluation of Literacy Campaign, Agra (UP), phase 1 and II" in Evaluation of Literacy Campaigns: Summary Reports, Vol. 1 (44-46) , New Delhi, Directorate of Adult Education, Govt. of India.

Mushtaq Ahmed (1994): Evaluation of Literacy Campaign, Almora, Lcuknow: State Resource Centre.

Muthuchamy (1992): A study of the Role performance of the Preraks, M.Phil. Dissertation, Alagappa University, Tamil Nadu.

NIRD (1994): Evaluation of TLC of Chittoor, Andhra Pradesh, Hyderabad, National Institute of Rural Development.

Nair, Omana and Rahim (1992): A study of the Programmes and activities of JSN organised by *Nehru Yuva Kendra* in Kerala, Trivendrum: Kerala Association for Non-formal Education and Development.

Om Mehta, Billore, Dave and Sharma (1994): " Evaluation of Literacy Campaign: Durg" in Evaluation of Literacy Campaigns: Summary Reports Vol.1 (12-13) New Delhi, Directorate of Adult Education, Govt of India.

Prem Chand (1993): Evaluation of Literacy Campaign in Dungarpur, New Delhi, National Institute of Adult Education.

Rokadiya, B.C. (1993): " Evaluation of Literacy Campaign, Ajmer", in Evaluation of Literacy Campaigns, *Summary Reports*, Vol. 1 (37-38), New Delhi: Directorate of Adult Education, Govt. of India.

Reddeppa (1993): A study of the Determinants of Prerak Effectiveness, M. Phil. Thesis, S.V. University.

State Resource Centre (1995): An Observational Study to identify the role of JSN in Continuing Education, Mysore, State Resource Centre.

TISS (1993): Evaluation of Literacy Campaign, Lathur, Bombay, Tata Institute of Social Sciences.

Vasumathi (1992): A study of the organisations and functions of *Jana Shikshana Nilayams* under Area Development approach of the NLM in the colleges of Kannur district, Master Dissertation, Calicult University.

•••

INDEX